From Figures to Facts

From Figures to Facts

by Christopher Day

Illustrations by Larry

'Read not to contradict and confute;
nor to believe and take for granted;
nor to find talk and discourse;
but to weigh and consider.'

Francis Bacon
Essays or Counsels Civil and Moral

Published by the King's Fund on behalf of the NHS/DHSS Health Services Information Steering Group

© Crown copyright 1985

Typeset by Bookworm Typesetting, Manchester

Printed and bound by Redwood Burn Ltd, Trowbridge, Wiltshire

Distributed for the King's Fund by Oxford University Press

ISBN 0 19 724627 3

King's Fund Publishing office
126 Albert Street
London NW1 7NF

Preface

The chief aim of this book is to assist members of health authorities to perform their function more effectively and to discharge their role with greater confidence and satisfaction. The author explains – in simple and clear language – the value and use of statistical information as an important management tool. He also shows how the content, organisation and presentation of data can illuminate the goals which an authority sets itself and the way it intends to achieve them.

The examples in the text are intended to demonstrate both the potentialities and the limitations of statistics and will find an echo in the problems encountered by all those concerned with the planning and delivery of health care. The book will thus be of interest not only to health authority members, but also to members of community health councils, to budget holders of all disciplines and to any other reader who wishes to evaluate the arguments of health care providers and decide for himself on their validity.

There can be little doubt that the present volume fills a widely acknowledged need; beyond this it is hoped that it will encourage the reader to explore the subject of management information further and apply his new found knowledge for the benefit of present and future users of the National Health Service.

Edith Körner
1985

Contents

	Preface	5
	Introduction	9
CHAPTER ONE	*Getting to grips*	15
CHAPTER TWO	*Waiting for hospital care*	27
CHAPTER THREE	*The use of hospital beds*	43
CHAPTER FOUR	*Plans and projects*	57
CHAPTER FIVE	*Manpower control*	77
CHAPTER SIX	*Comparisons between districts*	89
CHAPTER SEVEN	*Seduced by statistics: a cautionary tale*	99
CHAPTER EIGHT	*Words into actions*	113
POSTSCRIPT	*Figures, facts and general management*	121
APPENDIX A	*How to calculate the four common measures of bed use*	123
APPENDIX B	*Calculating a measure of bed use from two known measures and depicting all four measures on a single diagram*	125
	Index	131

Introduction

Do you help to provide health care? And do you suspect that you could perhaps be making better use of basic statistical information, if only you knew a bit more about it? If so, this book could well be of help to you.

It is addressed to members of health authorities in particular. If you are not one, press on regardless: the basic rules for using information are much the same, whatever your point of view.

How this book can help

Whatever your reasons for becoming an authority member, you probably had high hopes of making a contribution, however modest, towards the care and wellbeing of your fellow human beings in need.

Have you ever felt since then that the things you discuss seem to take you a long way from doing this? Most members find themselves having to readjust their thinking when they realise that the direct care and treatment of people in need has to be left entirely to the professionals, leaving members to deal with matters related only indirectly – often very indirectly – to these activities.

You may feel that the statistics you see are part and parcel of this remoteness from the scene of the action; that all those baffling figures bear little relevance to a service which above all is about providing for the individual needs of individual people. If that is how you feel, read on.

You will discover that, selected with understanding, presented intelligently and used purposefully, the information contained in those seemingly dry figures can lead you into taking action which directly and significantly improves the condition of those in need of care and those receiving it.

You may perhaps be worried that you know little enough about existing statistical information, let alone all the complexities about to be introduced with the computer revolution, the Körner* reports, performance indicators and the like.

---

*Mrs Körner was, until September 1984, chairman of a national working party looking at health service statistics. Chapter Eight outlines the implications of the working party's work.

10/From figures to facts

This book can still help. Its emphasis is on what is, not what may be. Of course, it looks to the future, but most of the measures it describes have been around for quite a time.

Some people – the fortunate few – are immediately at home with figures. Give them a table of statistical data, and away they go with their calculators, comparing, analysing and generally drawing erudite inferences.

You may not be so lucky: you may find the figures looking up at you blankly while you stare uncomprehendingly back, wondering if you are the only one to find them so totally meaningless and looking forward to moving on to discussing real people doing real things.

Whichever you are – at home with figures or all at sea with them – this book can help you.

Just as you can drive without knowing how a car works, so you can use numbers without knowing about statistical theory. This book is not about statistics: the few odd formulae it contains can safely be skipped. It is about using statistical information as a means of understanding more clearly what is going on, just as any other source of information is used, such as visiting a hospital, for example, or reading a report or taking part in a meeting. If you call the tune – by deciding what information you want and why, how you want to see it and when, what you intend to do with it – the mystique disappears, and you are left with a valuable aid to the tasks you perform.

One thing is for sure: demand for health care is increasing faster than our ability to satisfy it. The pressures on the service to stretch its resources, already much in evidence, will rise relentlessly as time goes on. It is only by knowing just how those resoures are being used and by exploiting that knowledge that we stand any hope of maintaining a responsive service. Information – sound, comprehensive, relevant and timely – forms the bedrock of that knowledge.

Against that background it is the responsibility of everyone concerned – not just the numerate minority – to understand and make use of the information that is expressed in the form of numbers.

That, above all, is what this book is about.

The recurring themes

This is not a theoretical textbook. It draws upon material from real life (appropriately disguised) and deals with issues which will be familiar to members once they have served on their authority for only a few months.

Some points are brought out only once or twice – though with a little imagination you will be able to think of many other situations in which they apply. Other points form the themes of the book and keep cropping up, especially:

Selection Members who decide for themselves what information they will see – with their officers' help – know why they are seeing it and what they will do with it. Members who let their officers decide for them have only a woolly idea why they are seeing it and what to do with it.

Presentation Your understanding of information is deeply affected by the way it is presented. There is simply no need for it to look obscure, confusing or dull.

Comparison Isolated figures mean very little. They need to be placed in the context of earlier figures – to distinguish trends – or of similar figures in other places – to assess relative performance.

What this book contains

Chapter One, an introductory chapter, explains why statistics are relevant to an authority's tasks. It describes the importance of selecting what to receive and the principles to bear in mind when making that selection. It emphasises the need to have information presented so that its important features can be readily grasped and to use it sensitively and constructively.

Chapter Two discusses waiting for hospital care, the measure of the balance between demand and a hospital's capacity to meet it. It underlines the importance of waiting times and describes the complexities of establishing them. It emphasises the importance of setting standards and describes the technique of exception reporting as a means of concentrating on the most worrying figures. And it explains what can happen to upset the balance between demand and capacity.

Chapter Three discusses the use of hospital beds. It concentrates on the four common measures of bed use, their strengths and their weaknesses. It explains how, by deciding in advance what figures it intends to interest itself in, an authority is by implication setting standards. It examines a recent bed use return and discusses how an authority went about deciding what figures it wished to see.

Chapter Four describes three techniques frequently used in planning: indexes, rates and norms; it then goes on to show how these and similar techniques were incorporated into a recently developed medical loan system.

Chapter Five examines an aspect of manpower statistics, manpower control, by looking at an authority's approach to a problem in its orthopaedic unit.

Chapter Six's theme is comparisons. Using a report on an impending crisis in a mental handicap hospital, it describes what an authority did to establish how the hospital compared with all similar hospitals in the country. The chapter describes how freely available statistical data has been assembled to allow such comparisons to be made, both within long stay hospitals and within most of the acute hospital specialties.

Chapter Seven uses a recent authority report to illustrate the importance of using statistics as an aid to analysing a problem, not as a substitute for that analysis. This report assembled certain statistics, omitted one crucial piece of statistical information, mistook the problem and led the authority into taking inappropriate action.

Chapter Eight looks forward to the implementation of the Körner recommendations and suggests how, collectively or individually, members can begin to make use of existing statistical information.

Before you begin

As you embark, beware! You could perhaps skim through this book in less than an hour, and those who already know a lot about statistics and are very quick on the uptake could perhaps absorb all it has to offer in that time.

You would probably find it better to take one chapter at a time, reflecting as you go on the way in which the ideas apply – or could be made to apply – in your district.

You may sometimes find it heavy going, though seldom obscure: jargon has been avoided as much as possible. The reward for your efforts will be a better understanding of what is going on and an increased ability to influence matters.

The ideas in the book have been developed by people with a long experience of health service management and have been found acceptable to members, staff and others from a wide background. But no claim is made that they are unique or special. As your familiarity with statistics grows, so will your confidence in handling them, and you will find yourself developing your own ideas, suited to your own district's special characteristics and your authority's views about them.

13/Introduction

CHAPTER ONE

Getting to grips

Why bother with statistics?

Not so long ago a newly appointed authority member decided to take a look around his local general hospital.

He went into a ward where he found that half the beds were empty. True, the staff seemed busy, but there appeared to be plenty of them about. He talked to a couple of patients who, he discovered, had been admitted only a few days after being seen in the outpatient department.

He came to the conclusion that there was really no pressure on this ward at all. Patients were being admitted almost at once, beds were under-occupied: clearly a case of too much being provided for the demand.

Imagine his surprise at the next meeting of the authority to find a report expressing concern about the pressure on this ward: occupancy levels were excessively high and the waiting list was long and increasing.

You probably realise what had happened. The new member had simply not appreciated that the beds were empty because several patients had just been discharged and that more were due to be admitted later in the day; nor had it occurred to him that the patients he had spoken to had been admitted quickly because they needed treatment urgently.

Of course, he could have looked in later on to see how many beds were occupied, and he could have asked *all* the patients how long they had been on the waiting list. Better still, he could have looked in every day for a month, counting the beds and talking to the patients: at the end of that time he would have been far more knowledgeable about the pressures on the ward.

Or he could have saved himself a lot of trouble and looked at the statistics.

Some people believe that statistics are about numbers. They are not. They use numbers,

16/From figures to facts

it is true, but only to describe in a form of shorthand what is happening to collections of people, things or events. In the health service the people are usually either patients – in their homes, in clinics, in hospital – or staff; the things are usually buildings, beds, meals, drugs and the like; the events are usually such things as clinic appointments, spells in hospital, tests, treatments, operations and so on.

Think of that new member: he arrived at a false conclusion because he discovered two things which, despite being true, were not in the least typical. He needed to enquire over and over again for the true picture to emerge. Statistical information does just that: it asks the same questions over and over again and assembles the answers to give pictures of what is happening.

If the right questions are asked, those pictures matter, because they can tell you things about your district's services which can be crucially important and which cannot be discovered in any other way: whether the services are responding to the needs of the people they serve; whether they are doing so promptly, effectively and economically; whether they are anticipating changes in those needs. And if you consider that your responsibilities extend to hundreds of thousands of potential customers, hundreds of staff and millions of pounds you will realise that you have no choice but to examine the many messages contained in those statistical pictures.

Clearing the decks

There is one certain way of making routine information seem consistently irrelevant, tedious and useless: all you need do is to go on receiving the same tired, dreary tables that you and your predecessors have been getting for no reason that anyone can remember since time began.

So put a stop to it without delay, and set aside an hour or two with your senior staff to decide, as an authority:

> What do we want to know?
> Why do we want to know this?
> What can give us this knowledge?
> What use do we intend to make of it?
> How do we want it presented to us?
> How often do we want it?
> When do we want to review what we see?

Structuring your thoughts in this way is just as important, whether you are considering the things you need to know routinely or whether you are considering what information you need to decide one particular issue. The crucial point is this: that as many of the authority as possible should develop a shared view of what they need to know, for what reason and with what aim. That achieved, the authority controls the information and is no longer – as is so often the case at present – controlled by it.

The next two sections assume that you and your authority colleagues have decided to meet to develop that shared view. They consider aspects of *selection* and then points about *presentation*. The emphasis is on routine information.

Selection

As you begin, be warned: it is temptingly easy to drift into rambling discussions about the meaning of health or some other such abstraction. Apply yourself to practical questions: Whom do you serve? Do they get the services they need? How are those services provided, and are they as good as you would like them to be? And be systematic in your approach.

What should you make your starting point?

Many erudite theories have been developed to describe the process of providing health services. The incredible jugular/funicular model of health care provision – a breakthrough in original thought, as you are bound to agree – is illustrated for the first time ever on page 18.

Too simple? Maybe, but it does highlight the five main stages in the provision of health care, each one of which is of potential interest and concern.

Stage 1 is the jug containing the *population* liable to need the health services, or one of them. It could be one of many populations: for community services, it would be the district's resident population; for maternity services, only women of child-bearing age; for geriatric services, just the people aged 65 and over, and so on.

Of course, these populations never remain the same for long. In the short term, for example, summer holidays can reduce the population of industrial towns and more than double the population of seaside resorts; in the longer term, fluctuations in birth rates over the years can cause major variations in the numbers in need of age-related forms of care; one of these – the growth in the number of very old people – is considered in Chapter Four.

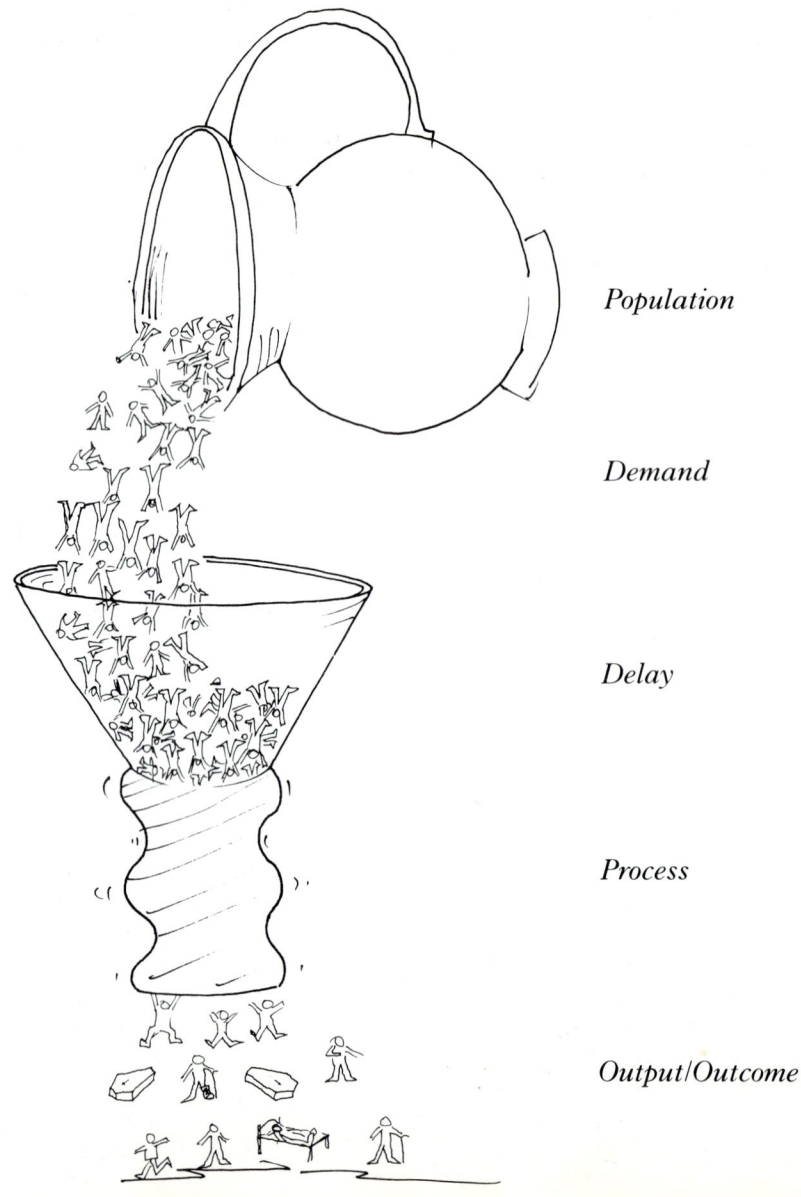

Many other factors – forms of employment, types of housing, the incidence of smoking, and so on – can also strongly influence the size of the population who may need particular forms of health care. The more you know about those you serve, the better will be your response to their needs.

Stage 2 – the flow of people from the jug – represents *demand* for services. It too is constantly changing. Some of the reasons for variations in hospital demand are included in Chapter Two.

Stage 3 is the bowl of the funnel, containing those who are *waiting* for the services they need. Again, Chapter Two discusses waiting for hospital care, but always remember that practically all the health care services involve delays. Those that do not – like the emergency services – are usually costly, as they involve making staff available for a level of demand which may not materialise.

Stage Four is the throat of the funnel, the *process* of providing the service. It is a huge throat, encompassing scores of different services and supporting activities. It is also highly complex and elastic: it needs to be held open wide enough to cope with the demand, but the efforts needed to keep it open – the staff, services, buildings and equipment, plus the managerial skills to keep them all in balance – are constantly opposed by pressures to restrict it, such as staff shortages, closures and financial restrictions. Chapter Three considers one particular aspect of this process, the use of hospital beds; Chapter Six considers an aspect of one of the resources, manpower control.

Stage Five is the outflow of people from the funnel, representing the number of people who have received the service (the *output*) and their condition (the *outcome*). As the diagram indicates, for some people it is the end of the process: they have been cured, or have obtained medication which will cure them, or perhaps they have not survived. For others, it is simply the end of a phase, and they are on their way into another funnel: the health care process is rarely confined to a single contact with the service. Indeed, where elderly people are concerned, contacts can run into hundreds, spanning many forms of service over many years. Your interest is likely to be in both the number involved – the outputs – and also the outcomes: the need for people to progress from one phase of health care to the next, and the factors that may hinder that progression.

Have your discussions encompassed the whole spectrum of population, demand, delay, process, output and outcome? If so, you are sure to be looking at a very long list indeed.

20/*From figures to facts*

Now is the time to move on to the second stage of the selection process: elimination. Here are some pointers:

How manageable?
Poised at the top of the pyramid, you need to have a broad view of virtually everything that is going on, so that you can immediately pick out anything that needs a more careful look: such things as the overworked ward described earlier on, for example, or the inadequacy of your chiropody services, or the low level of whooping cough vaccinations.

But you must be realistic: the time you can spend on authority matters is limited, and only a small proportion of it can be devoted to examining routine information. If you acknowledge at the outset that you are unlikely to spend more than perhaps 15 or 30 minutes a month on this information you will be defining one of the most important constraints on what you see.

Mind you, that is not the end of the matter. If you decide that you cannot cope with more than, say, five sets of information a month, they need not be the same five every month: you could, for example, decide to examine five different sets of information every month for six months – a total of 30 – and then begin again.

Other methods exist for cutting down the quantity to manageable proportions, such as exception reporting, described in Chapter Three.

How significant?
Given that you will have limited time to examine the information, you need to be sure that it is of broad significance in the context of all that is going on. You may have to accept for example that you will rarely or never be able to look at the levels of activity of some of the smaller departments (unless some specific problem arises in one of them), as the price for spending time on examining ways in which community nursing services and hospital beds are being used.

How useful?
Be sure that the information you select stands the test: is it within the authority's power to do something about it? If it is not, what purpose is served by having it?

How accessible?
Although a vast amount of information is collected, it is often not quite what an authority wants, or it is difficult to analyse or present in the form required. Even in the age of the computer, the practical difficulties of collecting and analysing data are

enormous, and although nothing is impossible you may be told that the complexities of obtaining it – not to mention the cost – put it out of court. A prudent authority might still like to have those complexities and costs defined!

How comparable?
Comparisons play a crucially important part in the examination of routine information. More often than not, what is compared is the performance of one particular unit or department over time: the number of patients treated last year, for example, compared with each of the five previous years.

Important though this is, there is another form of comparison which should never be overlooked: how your district's figures compare with those of other districts.

This is not always as straightforward as it may seem: there is little common agreement yet about the ground rules for making the comparisons, and one district's method of analysis – and the various elements that it puts in and leaves out – can differ considerably from another's. Standardising these ground rules will be one of the most important of the benefits of Körner, as you will see in Chapter Eight.

How easily evaluated?
Much of the routine information you select is likely to be presented to you in the form of relationships: patients treated per bed, for example, or expenditure per case, or cost per so many articles.

This is all to the good. Information that relates *inputs* – staff, accommodation, time, money – to *outputs* – numbers of patients treated, operations performed, home visits – is likely to be of more value than tables which simply show expenditure or staff in post on their own, as it allows you to see how much of the authority's resources is achieving how much of a return.

Presentation

You will probably want to rely on the skills of your expert staff to present you with the information you decide to see regularly. But remember that expertise brings its own risks, not least that you will not be able to make any sense of some chart or diagram which to the expert is perfectly clear. If you cannot follow what it is all about, protest! You will not be the only one, and it is the job of your officers to present information clearly.

This brings you to the first of several points about the presentation of information:

Display

There are usually better ways of displaying statistics than in tables of figures, as you will find as you work your way through this book. Pictures, diagrams, graphs and charts all have their place.

Black ink on white paper can achieve a great deal, but is well on the way out: colour is invaluable for simplifying the messages contained within complex displays: could it help you?

The chances are that there is a computer close at hand: it may be worthwhile to see what it can do. Chapters Four and Six describe several very useful computer applications, incorporating displays that can be understood very quickly and easily.

Accuracy

Some people tend to get very worried if they spot an inaccuracy or an incomplete statistic; and if it relates to their own work, they can quickly become very heated about it.

Understandable though this indignation is, you should think carefully before rejecting the information in response to it.

Accuracy is a relative term: it can matter a great deal if a doctor prescribes 20 mg instead of 2 mg; but it probably makes very little difference if home visits by community nurses are a few dozen out within a total of several thousand.

As you become more accustomed to looking at statistics you will find yourself growing more confident about them and developing a feeling about the 'rightness' of the figures.

Timeliness

You may often feel frustrated that the information you receive seems to be out of date. In some cases this can matter very much – particularly, of course, where revenue expenditure is concerned – but often it is much less important than it may seem.

Generally, a balance has to be struck between speed and accuracy, and it is for members to decide where that balance should be struck.

Inferences

It is only too easy to jump to a conclusion on the basis of statistical information, yet that conclusion may be quite wide of the mark. It is sensible always to have an interpretation of the information you receive and even then to regard it as no more than a starting point for further enquiries. Figures may be factual, but they rarely tell the whole story.

Averages
It is inevitable that most of the information you receive will be in the form of averages. Remember: averages conceal peaks and troughs. Just as a six-footer could walk into a river with an average depth of one foot and find the water over his head, so a ward with an average occupancy of 80 per cent could sometimes contain more patients than available beds.

Definitions
When comparing your district with others, remember that comprehensive rules do not exist for ensuring that common definitions are used, and those that do can be ignored or misinterpreted. One district was delighted that its inpatient bed use figures seemed so good – until it found that unlike all the others, it was adding in all its day cases!

Small numbers
Be very careful about small numbers: they can mean a great deal or very little.

An authority was appalled to learn that its figure of maternal deaths had increased by 100 per cent in the previous year – until it discovered that the actual number had risen from 1 to 2. Of course, that was two deaths too many, but it was not the major problem that the authority initially believed it to be.

In another case, an authority ignored as unimportant the fact that one of its major specialties had a turnover interval of 2.3 days, compared with a regional average of 1.5 days. It failed to appreciate that even that small difference meant 200 fewer patients going through the unit every year.

Misleading presentations
There are many ways in which information can be presented to exaggerate or understate the true position. Your staff will know them all and will understand when you say that you do not want them employed. A book has been written about them*: if you are avid for more when you have finished this book, why not read it?

Conclusion

One last word of caution before you move on. Statistical information is a powerful brew. It usually involves making comparisons, and very often those comparisons seem to imply

---

*How to Lie with Statistics, D Huff, Pelican Books, 1973.

24/From figures to facts judgments about staff. Even when such comparisons are favourable this can be a very sensitive subject: after all, the staff are not engaged in a competition to see who can treat the most patients; their job is to bring their skills to bear on patients who need them, and they can understandably feel resentful about comparatively uninvolved laymen descending from a great height with their fists full of figures.

Enquire you must: that is an important part of your role. To do so without arousing hostility is an essential skill if your staff are to appreciate that you share their interest in bringing the best possible care to those in need.

CHAPTER TWO

Waiting for hospital care

If you and your authority colleagues take time to consider what you need to keep yourselves informed about on a regular basis, the chances are that high on your list will come the time it takes for people to obtain hospital care: indeed, many authorities are regularly told how long people are having to wait for their first outpatient appointment and how many are awaiting admission.

You may have been told that waiting times and waiting lists are measures of demand on hospital services. They are not. They are measures of a balance: the balance between *demand* for a hospital service on the one hand and the service's *capacity* to meet that demand on the other. If they both increase together, waiting is unaffected; but if demand increases or capacity diminishes, up go the number of patients waiting and the time they wait.

People sometimes tend to think of these two elements – demand, and the capacity to meet it – as more or less static: a stable population, and a hospital with a fixed quantity of beds and other facilities. The truth is, however, that all sorts of factors are constantly operating on both sides of the equation, enough to cause large changes in waiting times and often to make them unacceptably long.

Obviously it matters very much that people should get the attention they need as promptly as possible. Health authorities can make things happen which will reduce waiting, but before they take action they must be able both to recognise when waiting is excessive and to understand what is causing it. Both these tasks are easier said than done, and they are what this chapter is about.

Section 1, Understanding hospital waiting, examines the need for waiting and explains the distinction between the time people wait and the number waiting. It stresses the importance of setting standards. It considers the impact of emergency cases on waiting and the division of lists into urgent, non-urgent and very urgent cases.

Section 2, Presenting the information, stresses the need for the information to be clear and relevant and to include explanations. It discusses exception reporting as a means of concentrating on excessive delays.

Table 1 Marchmain Health Authority
Outpatient clinics as at 30 June 1982: approximate waiting periods for new non-urgent patients (March waiting times in brackets)

Specialty	Consultant	St Sebastian's Hospital		St Julia's Hospital	
General medicine	Dr A	6 weeks	(6)	No clinic	
	Dr B	2 weeks	(4)	No clinic	
	Dr C	2 weeks	(2)	No clinic	
General surgery	Mr D	3 weeks	(3)	No clinic	
	Mr E	4 weeks	(7)	No clinic	
	Mr F	4 weeks	(3)	No clinic	
	Mr G	9 weeks	(5)	No clinic	
Chest medicine	Dr H	1 week	(1)	No clinic	
Dermatology	Dr I	2 weeks	(2)	No clinic	
Paediatrics	Dr J	10 weeks	(6)	6 weeks	(10)
	Dr K	3 weeks	(6)	12 weeks	(12)
Rheumatology	Dr L	7 weeks	(4)	No clinic	
Neurology	Dr M	11 weeks	(9)	No clinic	
Orthopaedic	Mr N	14 weeks	(12)	No clinic	
	Mr O	13 weeks	(18)	No clinic	
	Mr P	13 weeks	(12)	3 months	(3)
Ophthalmic	Mr Q	12 weeks	(8)	No clinic	
	Mr R	13 weeks	(9)	No clinic	
Gynaecology	Mr S	10 weeks	(19)	No clinic	
	Mr T	10 weeks	(14)	No clinic	
	Mr U	23 weeks	(21)	No clinic	
ENT	Mr V	11 weeks	(10)	No clinic	
	Mr W	10 weeks	(9)	No clinic	
Plastic surgery and burns	Mr X	3 weeks	(2)	No clinic	
	Mr Y	4 weeks	(4)	No clinic	
	Mr Z	1 week		No clinic	
Dentistry	Mr AA	4 weeks	(3)	No clinic	
	Mr BB	8 weeks	(6)	No clinic	
Orthodontics	Mr CC	10 months	(10)	No clinic	
Psychiatry	Dr DD	No Clinic		1 week	(4)
Geriatrics	Dr EE	1 week	(2)	No clinic	

Specialty	Consultant	Cordelia Hospital	
General surgery	Mr D	2 weeks	(2)
	Mr E	4 months	(4)
General medicine	Dr A	6 weeks	(6)
Orthopaedic	Mr P	8 weeks	(6)
ENT	Mr V	6 weeks	(8)
Gynaecology	Mr T	10 weeks	(8)
	Mr U	8 weeks	(8)
Paediatrics	Dr J	6 weeks	(8)

Section 3, Identifying the problem, describes the need to check the accuracy of waiting lists and explains how to discover whether increased demand or reduced capacity is the cause of increased waiting.

Section 4, Conclusion, stresses the importance of taking action when waiting times are excessive.

Section 1 Understanding hospital waiting

The first thing to accept is that there must be some waiting for hospital services, other than in cases of emergency. Waiting regulates what would otherwise be a completely haphazard flow of people to hospital and ensures, for example, that there are never staff sitting about on the off-chance that patients will turn up, or that a ward is not so crammed full that there is no room for emergencies.

So your concern as a member is that waiting should not be excessive, not that there should be none at all.

There are major differences in approach to patients awaiting their first outpatient appointment (currently called new outpatients or referrals) and patients awaiting admission (inpatients), and they will be treated separately in the next two parts of this section.

1 Outpatients
Have a look at Table 1, taken from the papers of a health authority not long ago. It is fairly typical of many such tables, and it is quite possible that your authority receives

30/From figures to facts

something of this sort. Very often it is prepared primarily to tell general practitioners how long their patients are likely to wait before being seen in outpatients.

As you can see, patients in this particular district may have to wait any time up to ten months, according to the specialty and consultant concerned.

What, then, is a reasonable wait and what is excessive?

First of all, you do not need to be concerned about the *clinical* need of patients: the general practitioners and consultants between them generally take care to ensure that people who need attention urgently are seen quickly. Table 1 has ignored the urgent cases, as the heading makes clear.

So you come in where there is no clinical urgency, where it is a question of saying, as a responsible authority with standards to uphold, we believe that the longest that anyone should have to wait for an outpatient appointment is: well, what? You, along with the people who sit around you at the board room table, *are* the authority. What do you think is reasonable?

You are in the business of setting standards. Of course, you may prefer not to stick your neck out and say anything at all. But if you do, you could be thought to have no opinion, or at least to be ducking the issue.

It really is no good for an authority to decide to keep an aspect of the service such as waiting time under review, without its members having a shared view of what is acceptable to them and what is not; and if they keep that view to themselves, they can scarcely be surprised if the providers of the service behave as though it did not exist.

So why not be bold: announce as an authority – after seeking the views of all concerned – what you regard as the longest time that an outpatient should have to wait, and make it clear that you will be taking an interest in times which exceed it.

Which of the clinics in Table 1 have excessive waiting times, would you say?

2 Inpatients
Table 2 – another real-life illustration – shows how many inpatients (and also day cases) are awaiting admission.

Members sometimes wonder why they are told how long patients are having to wait for

Table 2 Marchmain Health Authority
Comparison of inpatient waiting lists, 1982-1983

	June 1982 m	f	c	Total	Day cases	September 1982 m	f	c	Total	Day cases	Quarter ended December 1982 m	f	c	Total	Day cases	March 1983 m	f	c	Total	Day cases	June 1983 m	f	c	Total	Day cases
General medicine	4	3	–	7	–	–	–	–	–	–	–	–	–	–	–	–	–	–	10	–	2	1	–	3	–
Paediatrics	–	–	–	–	–	–	–	–	–	–	–	–	–	–	–	–	–	–	–	–	–	–	–	–	–
Chest medicine	–	–	–	–	–	–	–	–	–	–	–	–	–	–	–	–	–	–	–	–	–	–	–	–	–
Dermatology	1	2	–	3	–	–	2	–	2	–	2	2	–	4	–	1	1	–	2	–	2	1	–	3	–
Rheumatology	27	71	–	98	1	36	80	–	116	5	41	94	–	135	9	39	95	–	134	8	38	98	–	136	2
Geriatrics	9	19	–	28	–	2	10	–	12	–	2	5	–	7	–	3	10	–	13	–	4	10	–	14	–
General surgery	787	409	–	1196	347	802	430	–	1232	343	786	425	–	1211	334	803	464	–	1267	361	758	449	–	1207	332
Orthopaedics	190	527	86	803	191	204	534	53	791	190	212	529	51	796	219	267	605	46	918	259	234	557	30	821	280
Dentistry	60	111	60	231	211	60	107	55	222	213	72	108	39	219	237	83	126	44	253	228	77	143	65	285	185
Ophthalmology	72	127	17	216	65	52	79	12	143	78	46	133	23	202	118	69	124	22	215	88	58	127	31	216	80
Gynaecology	–	293	–	293	54	–	286	–	286	56	–	282	–	282	58	–	243	–	243	44	–	317	–	317	59
ENT	163	109	368	640	146	156	101	447	704	190	166	83	453	702	197	162	87	512	761	306	175	102	521	798	254
TOTALS	1313	1671	531	3515	1015	1312	1629	567	3508	1075	1327	1661	566	3558	1172	1427	1755	624	3806	1304	1348	1805	647	3800	1192

their first outpatient appointment but not how long they are waiting to be admitted; instead they are told how many are on the waiting list. The reason is really quite straightforward: patients who are referred to outpatients can immediately be given an appointment, a definite number of weeks ahead; but patients for admission can rarely be given a definite admission date and so are simply put on a waiting list instead.*

Fine, you may say, hotfoot from having just decided what constitutes an excessive outpatient waiting time, what is a reasonable number to have on an inpatient waiting list?

But of course you do not, because you know that however much your staff may toil away at producing dazzling displays of numbers such as in Table 2, your concern is not so much with *how many* people are waiting but *how long* they have to wait. And you do not have to be an Einstein to realise that a waiting list twice the length of another does not mean double the waiting time: the number of available beds, the length of stay, the proportion of emergency cases, the level of use by day cases, to name but a few, all crowd in to obscure the issue.

* But not always. A few consultants do give their patients definite admission dates and then claim, quite truthfully, not to have a waiting list at all. Be sure you receive details about all the patients who are waiting, whether or not they have been given an admission date.

32/From figures to facts

And they obscure it so much that tables like Table 2 are really of very limited use: if you follow a line for a particular specialty and see that the waiting list has increased, the chances are that waiting time has also increased (though by how much you can have no idea). But it would be quite unrealistic to assume that because the waiting list in Table 2 for orthopaedics (821) and ENT (798) are about the same length the patients are having to wait about the same time before being admitted; or that dental day cases are waiting three times as long as gynaeology day cases, simply because at 185 the dental day case waiting list is about three times gynaecology's 59.

So one thing quickly becomes clear: it is almost pointless for authorities to be told how many patients are on the waiting list. There must instead be some system for describing how long those patients are having to wait: and that is far from straightforward.

Emergency Admissions
Begin by considering how patients are admitted: with a few exceptions, either they go in as emergency admissions* – via the accident and emergency department, or sent straight in by their general practitioner – or they are seen in outpatients, where the consultant decides they should be admitted.

Clearly there is no need to worry about the waiting time of the emergency admissions. But they cannot be ignored, because every such admission takes a bed which otherwise would be occupied by a patient seen in outpatients; and although in some specialties emergency admissions account for only a tiny proportion of the total, in others – particularly general medicine and trauma and orthopaedics – they comprise perhaps eight or nine out of every ten patients admitted. Or to put it another way: if your orthopaedic unit has 70 beds, the chances are that fewer than 15 of them will be available for patients from the waiting list.

Admissions from outpatients
Now consider the patients seen in outpatients. Some will not need to be admitted at all. Of the rest, a few will need to be treated as emergencies and admitted at once. Most will be put on the waiting list, and if the staff know that all such patients will be admitted within a month or so, that will be that: they will not worry, and you do not need to either.

The problems begin when waiting times start to stretch into the more distant future: it is then that the medical staff feel they must distinguish between the urgent and non-urgent

---

* Sometimes called immediate admissions.

cases. If no more than a handful of patients are classified as urgent the problem may be held in check. But this is what can happen: the urgent cases jump the queue; as a result, the waiting time of the non-urgent cases increases; because of this increase, more patients are classified as urgent; these urgent cases jump the queue, and the waiting time of the non-urgent cases increases still further. A new phenomenon now emerges: so many patients are now being classified as urgent that some of them are having to wait longer than they should. To combat this a new classification, very urgent, is invented. And away goes the whole process once again, with the admission date of the non-urgent patients gradually disappearing over the horizon and into the land of sometime, never.

How do you pick up whether this is happening and how far it has gone?

Once the Körner recommendations are put into effect it will be possible to see at a glance how long every patient discharged in the previous year or quarter had to wait before being admitted; and how long every patient still due to be admitted has been waiting so far. In the meantime, every hospital has to keep a record which, for all its limitations, provides a useful indication of excessive waiting. That record is, for each specialty:

i   the number of urgent cases waiting for more than one month;

ii the number of non-urgent cases waiting for more than one year.

You may believe that the second of these measures in particular is far too lax and that no patient should have to wait longer than some much shorter period: fine, and if your district's record systems are up to it and the cost of extracting the information can be met, go ahead. But before you do so, just have a look at the figures that are already available in those two existing categories. It could be that you will find yourself with enough on your hands to keep you occupied for some time to come.

As you can see, inpatient waiting is fraught with complexities, and even now you are looking at *numbers* of patients and the time they *have* waited, rather than how long a patient is likely to have to wait, having been put on the waiting list today. Ways do exist to calculate this: if you decide to explore them, be sure that they take full account of the delaying effects which emergency and urgent cases have on the non-urgent patients. Many do not.

Section 2   Presenting the information

1 Outpatients
Look again at Table 1 (pages 28-29): quite a galaxy of information. Over 30 consultants, over 40 clinics, three hospitals; waiting times, now and three months ago.

34/From figures to facts

A pity perhaps that Cordelia Hospital has not been placed beside the other two, that a few waiting periods have been expressed in months and the rest in weeks and that 'No clinic' has been repeated quite so many times. But never mind: it is easy enough to pick out the waiting times that are longer than you would like them to be.

But how long have they been like that? And are they getting worse, or are they improving? You can see how they stood three months ago, but two figures are obviously not enough to indicate trends. Of course, you can look out your papers of six months before, but just where did you put them? Or did you throw them away?

Try again. There is clearly enough space for one column of figures in brackets. How about three or four?

Well, maybe. But is there not just a risk that with all those rows and columns of figures you might overlook something important? Besides, are there not going to be quite a few that need not concern you anyway?

And that is the clue to a very simple little technique which has been glorified by the title 'exception reporting'. Rather than looking at everything, you say, 'Report only the matters that are of potential concern to the authority', stating just what they are and how they are to be reported.

In the case of Table 1, the authority might have instructed its officers to report, in the form of graphs covering two years, all the clinics at which waiting time for new non-urgent patients exceeded six weeks at the end of both the last two quarters. Immediately they have excluded 25 of the clinics from consideration; but they have ensured that they obtain considerably more information about the 17 that remain, in a form far more readily understood than a table of closely packed figures could ever be.

Figure 1 shows how such a report could be displayed. You will see that there is even enough space for explanatory notes.

2 Inpatients

Table 2 (page 31) is a good illustration of a statistical table brim-full of information irrelevant to an authority's needs. Authorities are simply not in the business of drawing inferences from the relative proportion of males, females and children on waiting lists; and although trends are of interest they are difficult to distinguish when they demand that you leap several columns at a time to follow them.

Figure 2 (page 37) shows how trends show up far more clearly when displayed

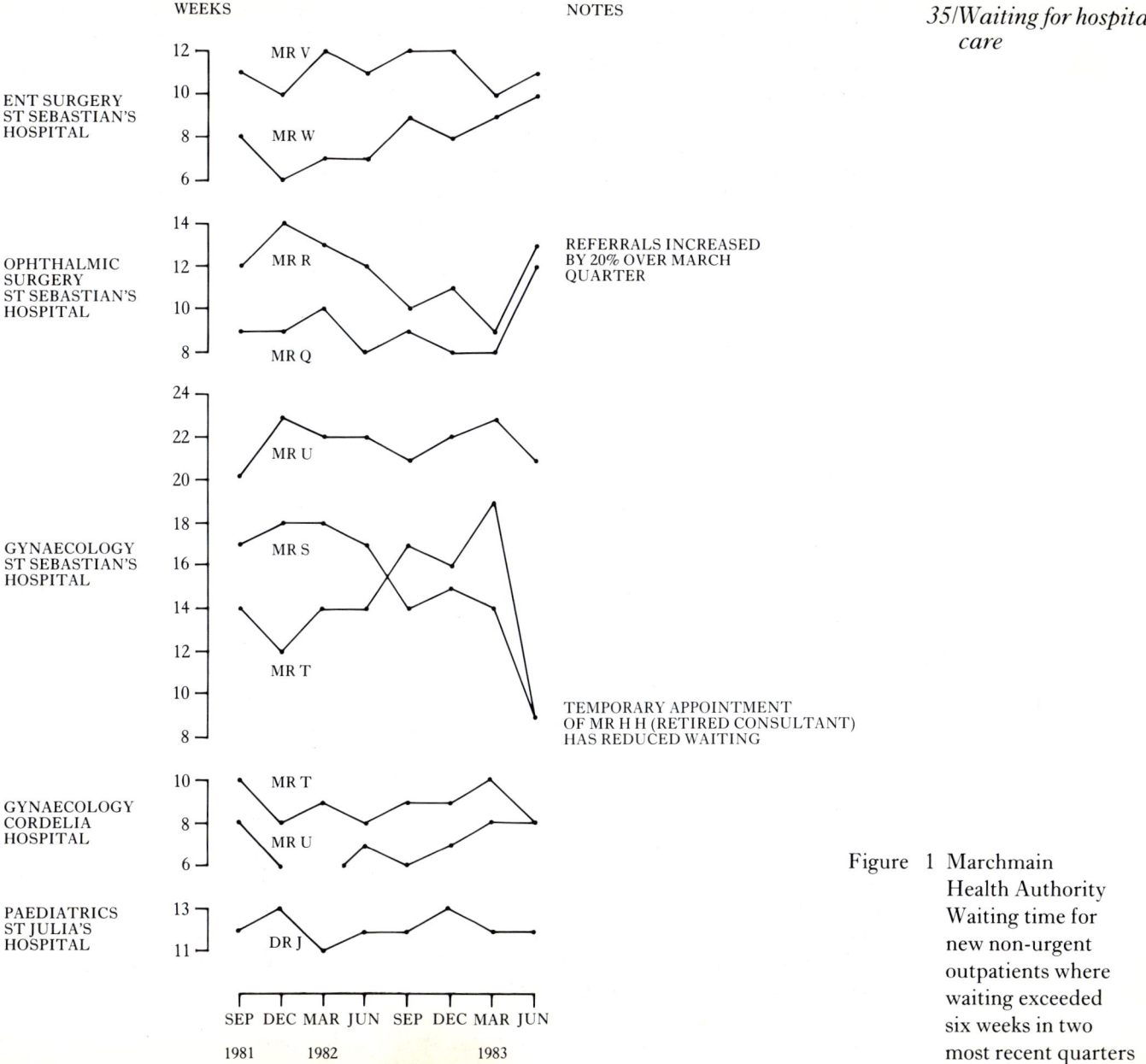

Figure 1 Marchmain Health Authority Waiting time for new non-urgent outpatients where waiting exceeded six weeks in two most recent quarters

36/*From figures to facts*   Figure 1 continued

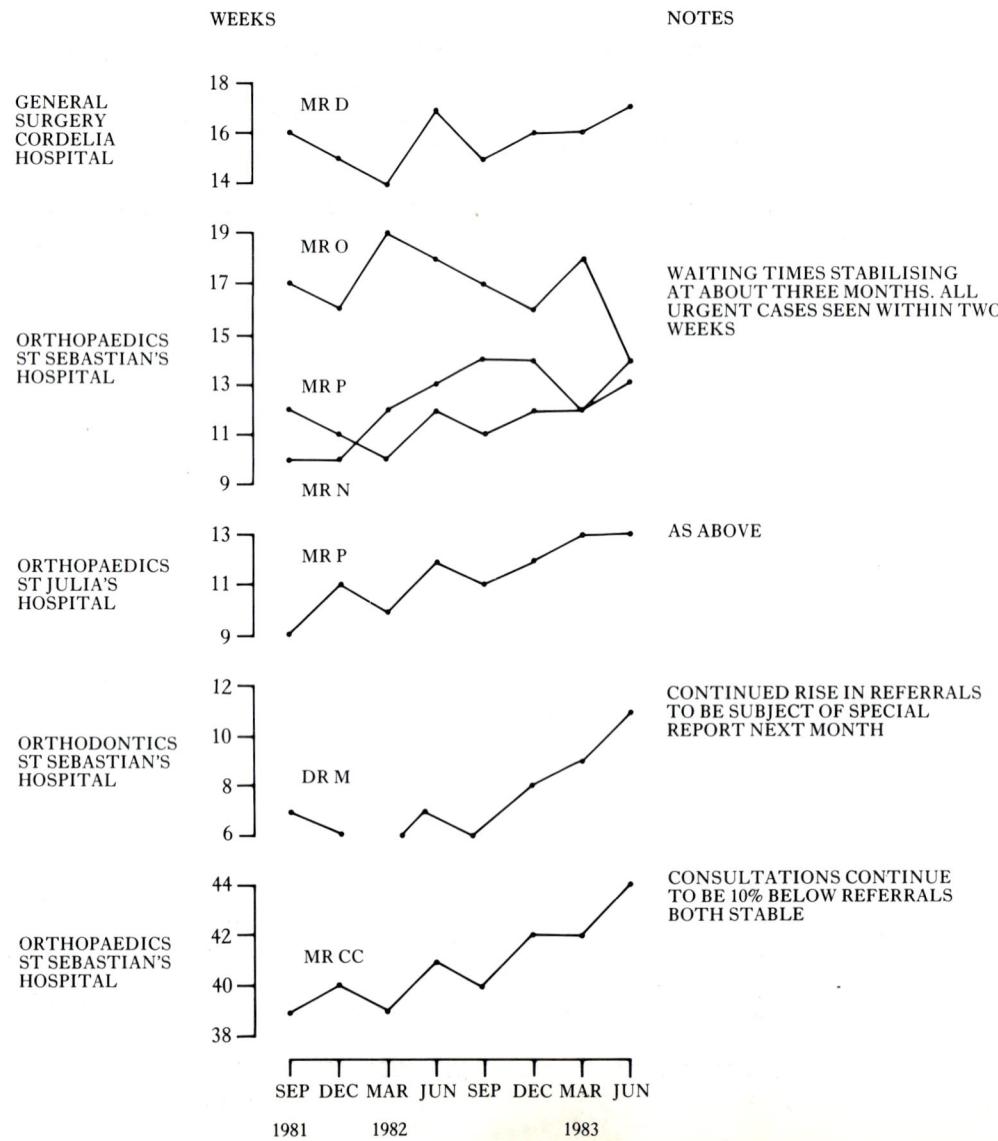

graphically; but it is included without enthusiasm, and only for the benefit of readers who cannot be persuaded that crude waiting list totals are of very limited value. (But can you spot the use of exception reporting?)

37/*Waiting for hospital care*

If, having considered the previous section, you decide to receive details of patients waiting in excess of one month (urgent cases) and one year (non-urgent cases) do bear this in mind: your main concern is not *how many* patients are waiting in excess of these periods, but the very fact that there are any waiting this long at all.

The numbers are useful only in that they indicate, when plotted over time, whether the problem seems to be reducing, staying the same or getting worse.

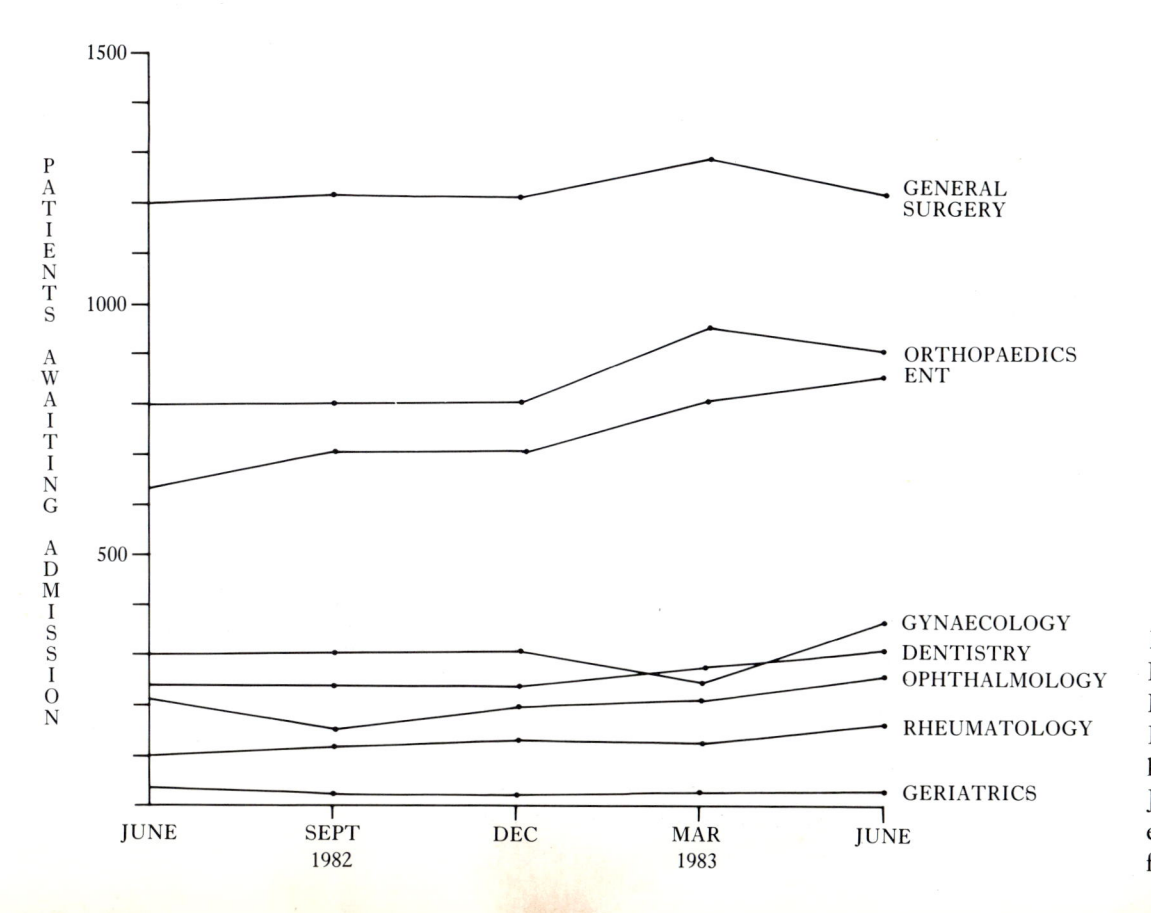

Figure 2
Marchmain Health Authority Inpatient waiting lists, last day of quarters June 1982 to June 1983, excluding lists of fewer than ten patients

38/*From figures to facts*   Figure 3 shows how graphs can be used to demonstrate what is going on; and taken with Figure 1, you have a broad overview of the problem areas in your district's hospitals. Where do you go from here?

Figure 3 Marchmain Health Authority
Patients awaiting admission: urgent cases waiting over one month and non-urgent cases waiting over 12 months*

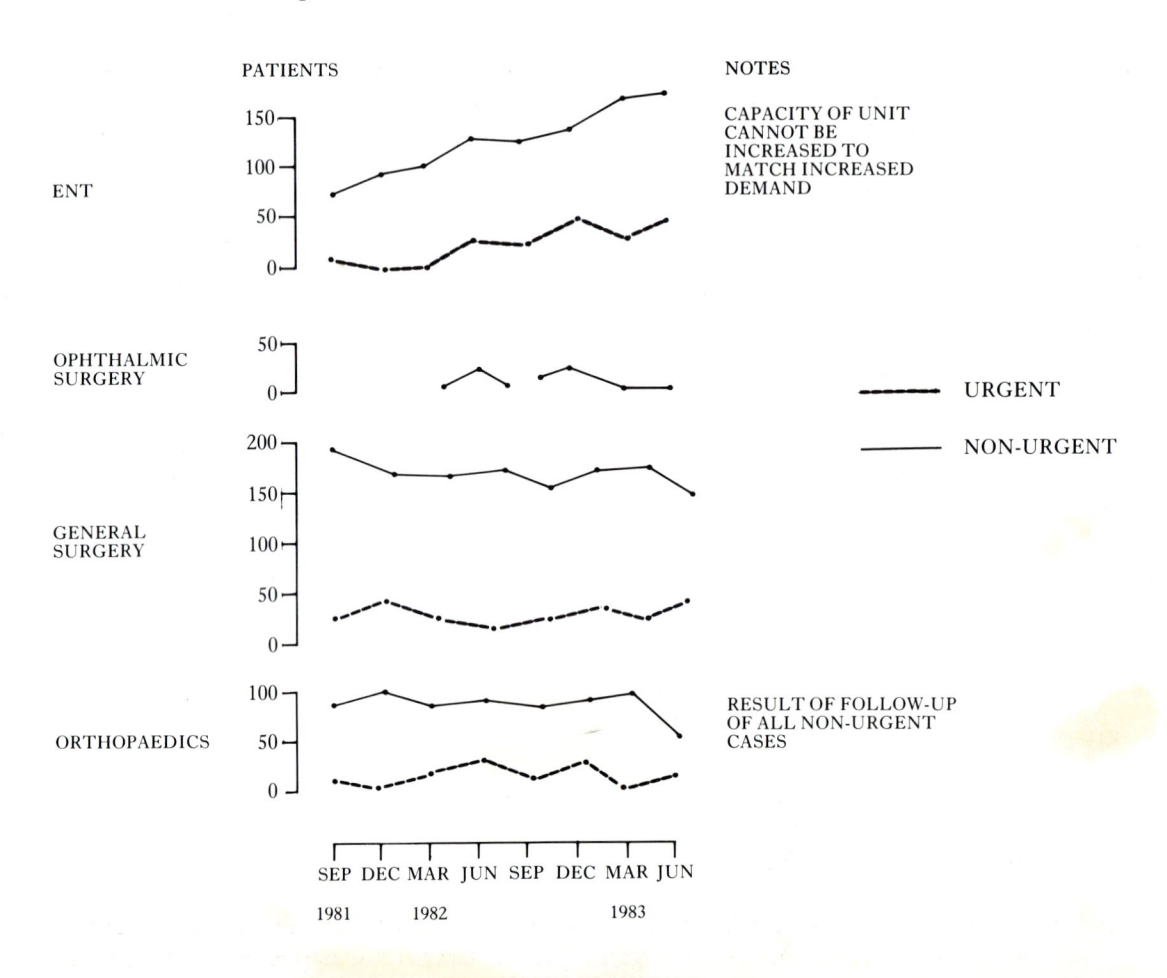

PATIENTS

ENT

NOTES

CAPACITY OF UNIT CANNOT BE INCREASED TO MATCH INCREASED DEMAND

OPHTHALMIC SURGERY

——— URGENT

——— NON-URGENT

GENERAL SURGERY

ORTHOPAEDICS

RESULT OF FOLLOW-UP OF ALL NON-URGENT CASES

SEP DEC MAR JUN SEP DEC MAR JUN
   1981   1982   1983

*EXCLUDING NON-URGENT CASES DECLINING ADMISSION

Section 3 Identifying the problem

You need to begin by checking whether there really is a problem at all. The first part of this section is about *accuracy*.

That out of the way, you need to examine whether the problem is one of *increased demand* or *reduced capacity* to meet the demand. The second and third parts of this section deal with each of these factors.

1 How accurate?

Waiting lists are notorious for overstating the number of patients actually waiting to be admitted. When examined, they are often found to include patients who have moved away to another part of the country or on to the next world; patients whose condition deteriorated and who were admitted as emergencies; patients who have decided to put up with their condition rather than have it put right in hospital, and so on.

Remember that your concern is about patients who have not been *called* for admission. There are often names at the tail end of waiting lists who have been called, often more than once, but who have not been able, or have not wanted, to be admitted. These patients should be identified and excluded at the same time as the inaccuracies are being sorted out.

Once the Körner recommendations have been implemented, the outcome of every offer of admission and the reason for removing every patient from the waiting list will be classified.

2 Has demand increased?

Demand on a hospital service increases in one (or more) of three ways:

i   more people are sent by general practitioners for outpatient consultation;

ii more people are put on the waiting list for admission;

iii more people are admitted as emergencies.

Ask to see statistics, over time, of
 general practitioner referrals,
  the number of patients placed on the waiting list and
  emergency admissions;
and if they show an increase, listen carefully to the explanations for the increase. Bear in mind particularly that you are concerned not just with what *has* happened, but what is likely to happen in the future.

What are the causes of increased demand? They can be many and varied, but they will probably come within one or more of these categories:

i an increase in the susceptible population: for example, a growth in the number of elderly people will put pressures on most of the acute services besides a district's geriatric and psychogeriatric facilities;

ii an increase in the incidence of a condition: for example, the incidence of chest disease often soars during a long spell of very cold, wet weather;

iii advances in medical technology: for example, many patients with cardiac conditions who have been treated by their general practitioners with drugs may be treated surgically with greater success;

iv changed referral patterns: for example, general practitioners situated between two acute hospitals may decide to change the hospital to which they refer their patients.

3 Has capacity been reduced?
Whether or not there has been an increased demand on a service you need to establish whether the service's capacity has been reduced: it can easily happen that both increased demand and reduced capacity occur at once.

So ask to see statistics, again over time, of (new) outpatients and of total admissions; and again, listen carefully to explanations and to forecasts of the service's ability to cope with the demand in the future.

Reduced capacity can arise from advances in technology which involve patients in having to stay in hospital for longer. But the far more probable explanation is that resources have been reduced: either temporarily, because of staff shortages, industrial action or the closure of perhaps a ward or operating theatre suite or other clinical facility for maintenance work; or on a long term basis, perhaps because of financial problems.

Section 4   Conclusion

This chapter has described how to recognise where excessive waiting times exist and what further information you need to identify the causes.

Now it is up to you to consider what must be done to bring those times down to an acceptable level. It will not be easy and may well involve difficult choices, including the switching of resources from less heavily committed services.

The essential thing is that you do something: it is fatal to the standing of an authority to demand information, set standards, identify inadequacies and do nothing at all.

It may well be, given the difficult conditions in which the NHS is operating at present, that you decide that you eventually have to make a conscious decision to accept the situation, at least for the time being, or even to lower your standards. So be it: at least you have thought about the problem and decided something. But more often than not you will find that the positive interest of members in the problems faced by the staff, and a constructive approach towards seeking a solution, will in themselves achieve a great deal.

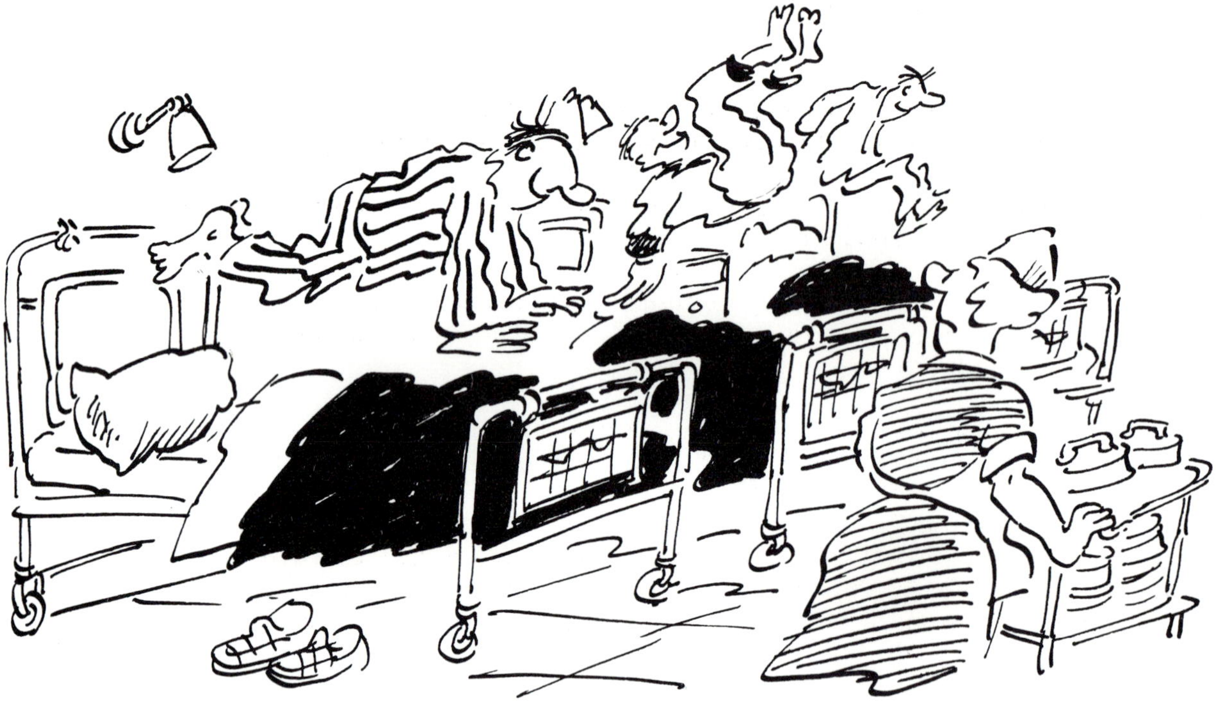

CHAPTER THREE

The use of hospital beds

In Chapter One you were recommended to set aside some time with the other members of your authority to discuss what figures you wish to see on a regular basis.

Some authorities, having thought long and hard, decide to receive information regularly about the use of the beds in their hospitals.

Why this emphasis on hospitals? Partly because hospitals are the heaviest health service spenders, and authorities are responsible to the government and the taxpayers for ensuring that their resources are properly applied.

But equally – even more so, many would argue – it is because members are concerned, not simply with the government and taxpayers, but with the occupants of those hospital beds. Consider: unlike everyone else in the population, most of them are seriously ill, desperately anxious, caught up in a strange and bewildering environment, heavily dependent upon the unfamiliar skills of complete strangers. With the help of sound information members can both ensure that the district's resources are used to good effect and also contribute materially to the well-being of the people who are in need of, and are receiving, hospital care.

Section 1, The tools of analysis, explains the four most common measures of bed use, describes how to assess them and discusses how to follow them up.

Section 2, Methods of presentation, examines a typical report on bed use and suggests how such a report can be made more useful.

Section 1   The tools of analysis

The four common measures of bed use concentrate on the use by *inpatients* of *available beds*.

Of the four measures, two are expressed in terms of time (days):

1   Length of stay
The average time that patients spend in hospital.

2   *Turnover interval*
The average time that beds stay empty between patients.

The two other measures are:

3   Percentage bed occupancy
How full on average the beds are being kept.

4   Throughput per bed
How many patients on average are passing through the beds.

As long as you can remember what these measures describe there is no real need to know how they are calculated: but for those who are numerate, interested or just keen to exercise their pocket calculators, the calculations are set out in Appendix A at the end of the book.

None of the measures tells a whole story: they are all simply indicators of areas to which to direct your attention. Length of stay, turnover interval and throughput are useful for assessing how intensively the beds are being used; percentage occupancy is of no help for this purpose, but it does tell you how full the hospital or ward is being kept. But do note: if you are given any two of these measures it is easy to work out the other two. Appendix B at the end of the book explains how; it also describes an ingenious diagram, called a Barber Johnson diagram, which sets out all four measures at the same time.

Each of the measures will shortly be examined, but first a warning about three things that often crop up and confuse the picture (they will all be sorted out once the Körner recommendations are put into effect).

Day cases Patients who go into hospital for a day, or part of a day, naturally add to the work of a ward, whether or not they occupy a bed, but they do not appear in the inpatient statistics. Be sure not to overlook these cases when you consider the workload of ward staff.

Flexibility of ward use When the present statistical systems were devised, individual specialties were allocated to individual wards. Nowadays the arrangements are far less rigid, and flexible allocations, bed borrowing and multi-specialty wards are common-place. This means that when a bed is empty there is no knowing which specialty 'ought' to have a patient in it, and nobody is very happy about the guidelines about deciding.

Because of this uncertainty you need to look very cautiously at bed use statistics based on specialties. If you know that flexible arrangements do exist, you may well do better to concentrate on statistics based on wards. True, wards cannot be compared across districts as specialties can, but as flexibility in the use of beds is now quite common the comparisons you lose are likely to be unreliable anyway.

Transfers within hospitals Most patients are discharged from the ward they were admitted to; but about one patient in every ten is transferred between wards before leaving hospital. Whenever this happens the average length of stay in the first ward is exaggerated (Appendix A explains how the method of calculation causes this).

Now for the four measures.

1 Length of stay
Length of stay describes how many days on average each patient stays in hospital: or to put it another way, it tells you how quickly people are being treated in hospital and returned home. Most people naturally want their stay to be as short as their condition will allow, and anything that prolongs it can only add to the stresses inseparable from being in hospital. On the other hand, of course, it can do a patient no good to be sent home too soon.

Suppose you are told that a hospital's ENT patients stay in for seven days. How do you judge whether this is too short, too long or just right?

Of course, patients generally stay in for as long as doctors decide they need hospital care, and you are in no position to judge those decisions. But what you can do is to make comparisons, with a neighbouring district, or with a regional or national average; and provided that you compare like with like – obviously you cannot, for example, usefully compare one specialty's figures with those of a different specialty – the information you obtain can form a valuable starting point for further enquiries.

Longer stays than average What then should you do if you notice that in a particular specialty length of stay in your local hospital is, perhaps, half as long again as the national average?

Simple: ask why it is.

Consider carefully what you are told. A quick explanation, in particular, is not always a complete or wholly accurate one.

46/From figures to facts

At the same time, take care to avoid implying criticism. Remind yourself that you are skirting prohibited territory: the stage at which to discharge a patient is very much a matter for the clinical judgment of the physician or surgeon concerned. And bear in mind too that conservatism, excessive caution or plain indifference on the part of those staff are probably the least likely of the causes.

So enquire, and you are likely to receive one or more of a great variety of reasons.

You may, for example, be told that the case mix within the specialty is not typical. There could perhaps be more people locally suffering from an illness requiring lengthy treatment than elsewhere; or the unit concerned has an expertise in treating particularly difficult conditions and therefore attracts a high proportion of people with these conditions; or perhaps a local private hospital is creaming off the minor cases, thereby pushing up the average length of stay of those admitted to the district general hospital.

Or you may learn that patients treated elsewhere as short stay inpatients are treated in your district as day cases: this removes them from the calculation and thereby exaggerates the average length of stay. Notice, incidentally, how this entirely praiseworthy practice, sparing patients the need to stay in hospital overnight, sends the figures in the wrong direction! (No need to write an indignant letter to *The Times*: the Körner recommendations will put this anomaly to rights.)

Reasons of this sort do not call for any intervention by the authority.

On the other hand, you may be told that emergencies are constantly disrupting theatre lists; or that great difficulty is being experienced in discharging elderly patients to suitable accommodation, or that the home nursing service is so overstretched that it cannot cope with patients requiring frequent attention. Now you can ask: why is this more of a problem for your authority than for others? And what scope is there for removing these bottlenecks from the system?

Or perhaps you may be told – or gather, or suspect, for want of a better explanation – that the demand for inpatient care is low and that patients are being kept in hospital because there are simply none to take their place. You may then ask: what can be done to improve the match between demand and supply?

Even these few possible responses suffice to show that a longer stay than average can arise from a wide variety of causes. Some call for action, some do not. You may even find some decreasing simply because the authority has shown an interest!

Shorter stays than average What of significantly shorter than average lengths of stay? They are just as worthy of a careful look. Some explanations may be the exact opposite of those that account for longer stays than average. For example, patients may be going into hospital for a night or two, when in other hospitals such patients are being treated as day cases; a sideways glance at the figures of day cases should yield a clue. But it could be that there is undue pressure on too few beds: you will soon be told if doctors are discharging patients sooner than ideally they would like.

Whatever you do, guard against the lazy simplification: shorter than average, good; longer than average, bad. Show your interest in all significant differences.

If you succeed in achieving an improvement – which it may be well within your compass to do – you will have the satisfaction of knowing that you have made an important contribution to the wellbeing of the patients concerned. If you are not able to, nothing will have been lost, and you – along, no doubt, with a good few of your fellow members – will have deepened your understanding of the complexities of bed use.

2 *Turnover interval*

Turnover interval: what a terrible piece of jargon! But you will do very well to get used to it, as it is an extremely useful measure. There is really nothing complex about it: just as length of stay describes the time between a patient's admission and discharge, so turnover interval describes the time between that discharge and the next patient's admission. A turnover interval of 2.5 days, for example, means that on average each bed was empty for 2½ days between the discharge of one patient and the admission of the next.

It has three particular advantages over the other three measures of bed use.

First, the time needed to get a bed ready for the next patient is much the same, regardless of the bed, the type of hospital or the specialty: so it is a matter of legitimate interest if, for example, the turnover interval in ENT surgery is twice what it is in gynaecology. Indeed, an authority could justifiably announce that it proposed in future to interest itself in all turnover intervals outside the range of, say, 1 to 2½ days. (Setting standards – do you recall this from Chapter Two?)

Second, it is a fair generalisation that the longer the turnover interval, the less satisfactorily the beds are being used, to the detriment of patients waiting to be admitted.

48/From figures to facts

Third, turnover interval is unrelated to questions of clinical judgment. It is true that beds are sometimes kept empty for clinical reasons (for example, because of an outbreak of infection); but when this happens the beds are closed, cease to be classed as available and no longer count in the calculation of turnover interval.

Be sure, then, to ask for the turnover interval figures, and show your concern about those that are considerably different from others in the district and from national or regional averages. And remember that when you are dealing with low numbers it does not take much for them to differ considerably: a period of three days may not seem a lot longer than two; but it is half as long again, and that is a very considerable difference.

> In 1982 the length of stay in a hospital's 90-bedded surgical unit was exactly the same as the regional average at 7.6 days; but its turnover interval was 2.4 days compared with the regional average of 1.6 days. Had the unit achieved the regional average turnover interval it would have admitted 285 more patients in the year.

Long turnover intervals You will find that there are two factors that frequently crop up to lengthen turnover interval.

One concerns specialist beds: these may be little used for long periods, but they still have to be kept available for a large influx of patients: typical examples are infectious diseases beds and special care cots.

The other factor is emergencies: where beds are kept available for emergency cases which do not materialise, turnover intervals are bound to be longer than they would otherwise be. But where this is the rule rather than the exception be sure to ask whether the unit is perhaps holding too many beds back for emergencies, particularly if waiting lists in the specialty are long.

Remember, you are fully justified in looking critically at long turnover intervals: they may mean that patients on the waiting list are having the distress, anxiety and often pain of waiting longer than necessary; they may also mean that staff are under-occupied, perhaps to the point of boredom and demoralisation, adversely affecting the patients in their care.

Short turnover intervals Exceptionally short turnover intervals are also a matter for enquiry. But do not stop at enquiring. Visit the unit concerned and see for yourself what is happening: you may find an atmosphere of calm, controlled efficiency; but you could find a harassed, anxious staff, reaching the end of their tether as they attempt to cope with an excessive workload: it has been known.

3 Percentage bed occupancy

This describes how full the beds in a ward, a hospital or a specialist unit have been kept; a bed occupancy of 75 per cent, for example, means that on average three-quarters of the beds were occupied in the period concerned. You may well have seen this measure or heard it quoted: it has been the staple statistical diet of health authorities ever since the earliest days of the NHS.

For all that, it should be treated with great caution. A simple example will explain why.

> The health authority of Malfrey District noticed that its thoracic unit's bed occupancy figure was 80 per cent, compared with 80 per cent in Lamstock District and 71 per cent in Granchester District. It concluded that all was well and moved on to other things.
>
> How wrong it was! Not only was it keeping its patients in hospital much longer than the other two districts, it was also leaving its beds empty between patients far longer.
>
> And what of Granchester, with its considerably lower bed occupancy level? It was sending its patients home much *sooner* than both Malfrey and Lamstock!
>
> If you find that hard to swallow, look at the figures in Table 3.

Table 3 Comparative statistics of bed use

	Bed occupancy %	Length of stay days	Turnover interval days
Malfrey District	80	12	3
Lamstock District	80	8	2
Granchester District	71	5	2

Malfrey had made a simple, but very common mistake: it had looked to the bed occupancy figures to tell it *how well* the beds were being used, whereas all they can describe is *how full* the unit is being kept – quite another matter.

This does not mean that bed occupancy figures are useless. Some people find it particularly helpful to turn them round, calling a bed *occupancy* level of 75 per cent a bed *emptiness* level of 25 per cent: certainly, saying that a ward has an average occupancy of 75 per cent does not have quite the same impact as saying that on average a quarter of its beds are empty every night!

But it is the easiest thing in the world to increase occupancy levels, simply by keeping patients in hospital longer than necessary, and that is no good to anybody. To know how *intensively* beds are being used you must examine one or more of the three other measures.

4   Throughput per bed
This measure tells you how many patients on average are admitted to each bed in, say, three months or a year: an annual throughput of, for example, 52 means that on average 52 patients are admitted to each bed in a year.

You may find it interesting to calculate the annual throughput of patients per bed in Malfrey, Lamstock and Granchester, using the formulae in Appendix B. Table 4 shows what you should find.

Table 4 Throughput per bed

	Patients
Malfrey District	24
Lamstock District	37
Granchester District	52

Fair enough, but what do you make of it? Granchester is clearly making the most intensive use of its beds, but how does this come about? Does Lamstock's less intensive use of its beds come about because its patients stay in hospital longer, or because the beds remain empty for longer between patients?

Throughput per bed is excellent for measuring how intensively beds are being used; but to discover the reasons for exceptional throughput rates you need to look at length of stay and turnover interval.

Section 2   Methods of presentation

Table 5 has been taken from the papers of a health authority.

This table is not being held up as a model of perfection: indeed, it is included because it contains numerous examples of statistics at their least helpful. But at least the authority is being told *something* about the way its beds are being used. Is yours?

Table 5 Kirkaston Health Authority
Bed occupancy return for March 1983

51/The use of hospital beds

		1	2 Available staffed beds	3 Average daily occupancy	4 % Occupancy March	5 % Occupancy February	6 % Occupancy January
		Hospital					
Hospital A			14	9.9	70.5	69.1	69.1
Hospital B	Acute		18	15.6	86.7	85.6	88.5
	Maternity		5	2.9	58.0	47.5	36.8
Hospital C			18	16.3	90.7	90.3	92.3
Hospital D	Acute		64	31.5	49.2	59.0	52.8
	Geriatric		131	118.6	90.5	92.9	91.6
	Maternity		15	7.1	47.1	36.0	25.5
Hospital E			22	16.8	76.3	71.8	71.1
Hospital F	Acute		42	29.9	71.3	71.3	70.0
	Geriatric		22	21.2	96.2	98.9	96.2
	Maternity		9	4.2	46.6	46.4	57.0
Hospital G			22	17.8	81.1	68.3	66.6
Hospital H	Acute		320	270.2	84.5	82.6	82.0
	Geriatric		28	26.5	94.7	92.5	91.1
	Maternity		20	11.7	58.4	54.1	52.7
Hospital J			12	10.5	87.1	88.4	82.3
Hospital K			85	80.5	94.7	96.9	92.9

Here are some observations on Table 5.

General   It is generally more useful for an authority to know how *intensively* its beds are being used, rather than how full they are being kept.

Comparisons with other districts, or with national or regional averages, would allow the authority to put the figures in perspective.

A *commentary* on or interpretation of the figures would help to explain them.

Main heading   The heading, referring to one month, is at variance with the table, which relates to three months.

Column 1   It would be more helpful to group the information by specialty

52/*From figures to facts*

rather than by hospital, as comparisons (except of turnover interval) between one specialty and another within a hospital are meaningless.

In four cases figures are provided against the entry 'acute'. A single occupancy level for a range of acute specialties is best avoided, as it is bound to encompass a whole range of levels between one specialty and another.

Column 3   Arbitrary fluctuations are bound to occur from one month to the next; they are much less of a problem if quarterly figures are used.

Columns 3-4   Columns 3 and 4 simply provide the same information in two different ways.

Columns 4-6   The months January to March are made to run from right to left; most people would find it more natural to read them from left to right.

Normally, comparisons over time are presented to indicate trends; but trends in occupancy levels cannot be inferred from figures covering only three months.

The decimal figures in these columns give a spurious impression of accuracy.

So what did the authority learn from this table? Only that some units were more fully occupied than others: hardly a surprising or illuminating conclusion.

Uninformative statistics are not merely valueless: they implant in people's minds the impression that statistics are by their nature obscure and irrelevant. You have seen that they need not be and that they can easily be made to draw your attention to matters which directly affect the care of patients.

A single, ideal, presentation exists no more for bed use statistics, however, than for any other body of information; and an authority must decide for itself, with help from officers who can guide it on questions of feasibility, what it wants to see, how often and in what form.

Table 6 shows the outcome of an authority's deliberations on these questions.

First, the authority decided it would see the bed use figures for its acute hospitals at

Table 6 Marston Health Authority
Bed use statistics: acute hospital specialties, first quarter 1983

Specialty		Available beds	Length of stay – days	Region	Turnover interval days	Day cases	Waiting list
General medicine	– Hosp A	12	10.0		2.2		0
	Hosp B	8	9.7		1.3		0
	Hosp C	84	11.5	10.5	3.1[3]	165	7
	Hosp D	15	10.3		1.5	15	0
	Hosp E	6	12.1		1.7		1
	District	125	11.1		2.8	180	8
General surgery	– Hosp A	16	7.7		1.6	5	140
	Hosp B	10	6.4		2.0	9	112
	Hosp C	65[1]	8.3	7.6	2.1	42	621[7]
	Hosp D	15	9.4[2]		4.0[4]	2	239
	District	106	8.2		2.3	60	1112
Trauma & ortho	– Hosp C	30	10.3		0.9	4	180
	Hosp D	12	9.1	8.8	0.8[5]		77
	District	42	10.0		0.9	6	257
ENT surgery	– Hosp C	15	3.2	4.0	2.5	19	344
Gynaecology	– Hosp A	48	2.9	3.5	1.4	34	512
Obstetrics	– Hosp C	50	4.9	5.0	1.9		–
GP maternity	– Hosp E	6	1.1	1.3	26.3[6]		
Paediatrics	– Hosp C	15	3.9	4.2	2.4	8	3
Dental surgery	– Hosp D	6	2.8	3.5	1.4		56
Ophthalmology	– Hosp D	7	7.0	8.8	2.5	22	147

Notes
1 Seven beds closed for ten weeks – staff shortages.
2 High proportion of major cases.
3 Large number of day cases exaggerate this figure.
4 Cause not yet identified.
5 Emergencies were 75 per cent of all admissions – normally under 70 per cent.
6 Low demand, as previously.
7 Previously 552. Bed closure – see 1 above.

quarterly intervals; and it decided that the specialties located in two or more hospitals should be grouped together for ease of comparison.

Next, it decided precisely what information to receive, and why:

1 Available beds: to be reminded regularly of the size of the specialty and to allow

members to make further calculations (for example, actual number of patients admitted, effect of adding in day cases) if they wished to do so.

2   Length of stay – district: to permit comparisons with

3   Length of stay – region.

4   Turnover interval: as an indication of the effectiveness with which the beds were being used.

5   Day cases: for their potential effect on inpatient bed use.

6   Waiting list: to relate numbers treated to numbers waiting.

Finally, it decided it wished to receive notes with these statistics each time, covering any noteworthy points about the use of beds, to include invariably:

Available beds: all reductions not approved in advance;

Length of stay: all variations greater than 20 per cent from the regional average;

Turnover interval: all intervals under 0.9 days and over 2.5 days;

Waiting list: all increases of more than 10 per cent on previous quarter;

Any other points about the use of beds considered by the officers to be worthy of note.

You will probably recognise that, although not defined as such, these requirements by the authority constituted standard setting. On length of stay, for example, the authority was saying by implication: we regard variations of up to 20 per cent above or below the regional average as acceptable. You will also notice that an onus of responsibility is placed squarely on the officers: they must identify, say, a 15 per cent rise in a waiting list over 12 months and then judge whether it should be brought to the authority's attention.

The general appearance of Table 6 may seem just as uninspiring as that of Table 5, but there is a huge difference between them. Table 5 was devised by officers and was based on their idea of what the members might like to see. Table 6 is the fruit of the members' own labours: they understand it, and they know what they are looking for within it.

Of course, your authority could discuss these questions and arrive at completely different decisions.

And why not? Having worked through the problem together, members will have deepened their understanding of the meaning of the statistics and will know what they are looking for when the figures are presented. That will be an enormous advance on what is happening at authority meetings up and down the country at present.

A last word of warning

Having mastered this chapter, you should have some basic ideas about what to look out for when you consider statistics about hospital beds.

It will nevertheless not come as an amazing revelation to you that people do not go into hospital to occupy beds, but to have their various troubles diagnosed, assessed, treated and (as far as possible) put right. Problems in that process can be reflected in the bed use figures, as you have seen, but they can just as easily not.

Be on your guard about this: first, and most important, get to know your hospitals and the people who work in them; second, look occasionally at the statistics of at least their major departments; third, take care not to assume that if the bed figures are satisfactory, all must be well.

If you would like to look further into these complexities you may be interested to read an absorbing book, *Hospital Beds* by J G Yates (Heinemann Medical 1982). There may well be a copy in your district offices or public library.

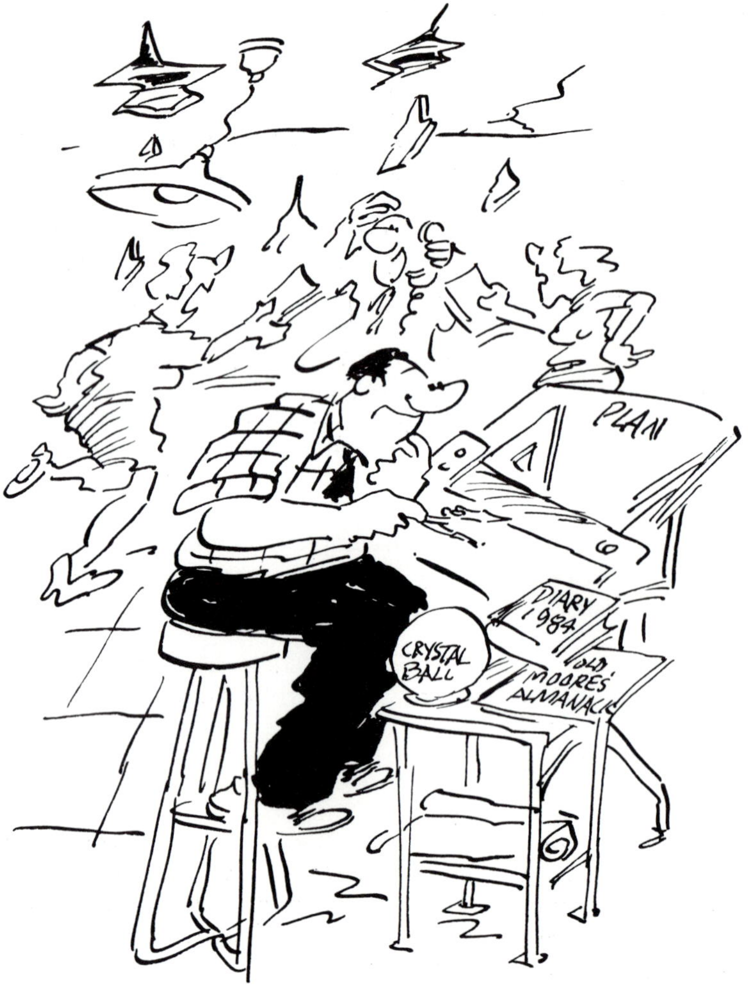
PLAN
DIARY 1984
CRYSTAL BALL
OLD MOORES ALMANACK

CHAPTER FOUR

Plans and projects

Once a year health authorities are formally required to look to the future. This happens when their district plans are presented for discussion and approval.

Do not be put off by the sheer size of the district plan. Remember that it is tackling one simple question: within the resources we expect to have, what should we be doing to improve services and to deal with impending changes in our district's needs?

This chapter is not about how to plan (a highly complex subject), but about the use that can be made of some simple, well known techniques for identifying major issues and for speeding up your understanding of complex data. It is in two sections:

Section 1 describes three such techniques often found in planning documents:

1 indexing
2 rates
3 norms

Section 2 describes how an authority introduced a system which makes use of those techniques and provides additional information about the way the service is being used.

Section 1 Techniques in planning

1 Indexing

Most people are familiar with the retail price index. The current index started in January 1974. At that time, the prices of several hundred goods and services were collected and then adjusted in various ways to reflect the way in which people were spending their money. Whatever figure resulted from all these calculations was scaled up or down to become 100 – the starting figure for almost all indexes.

Once a month thereafter the same calculations have been performed, and gradually the index has gone up until by January 1984 it stood at 342.6. Its meaning: generally that the goods and services which cost £100 to obtain in January 1974 would cost £342.60 to obtain in January 1984. (If you are an expert on the subject you will know that it is not quite as straightforward as this.)

58/*From figures to facts*   Figure 4   Marchmain Health Authority
Elderly population by age, 1981-1991

SOURCE: COUNTY PLANNING DEPARTMENT

59/*Plans and projects*

Indexes can be used to highlight trends in many aspects of the health service. The example below shows how population trends can be indexed to bring out changes which might otherwise go unnoticed.

The case of the elderly residents

In 1981 Marchmain Health Authority contained 26 000 residents aged 65 and over. This figure was expected to rise to 27 200 in 1987 and then return to 26 000 in 1991.

Until a few years ago, that would have been the end of the matter, and the change would have been shrugged off as being of no consequence. But people now realise that it is important to examine just how old the people within that total really are, because the older they become, the more they call upon the health services. Figure 4 shows this by breaking the total into three groups: those aged 65-74, 75-84 and over 85 years old.

If you look carefully at Figure 4 you may be able to spot a particular feature contained within it. But most people would see nothing very significant beyond a slight fall here, a small rise there.

It is in this sort of situation that indexing can be especially useful.

Figure 5 shows the *indexed* population of elderly people. The line on the graph has

Figure 5 Marchmain Health Authority
        Elderly population, 1981-1991

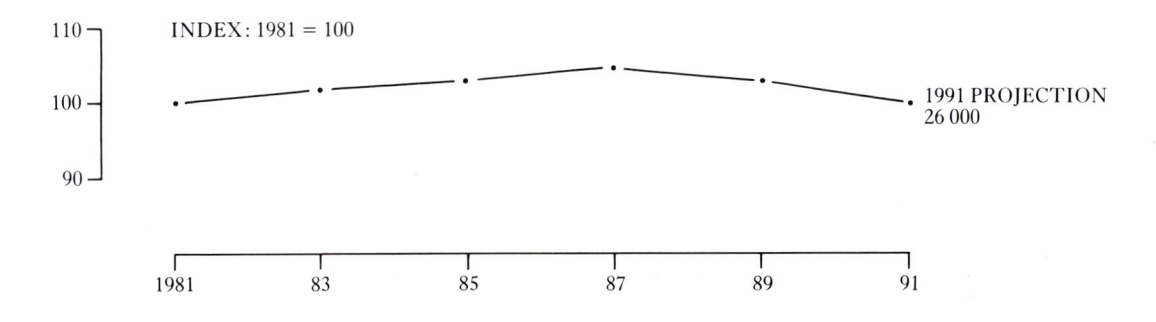

INDEX: 1981 = 100

1991 PROJECTION
26 000

SOURCE: COUNTY PLANNING DEPARTMENT

much the same shape as the top line of Figure 4. But instead of starting and ending at 26 000, with a rise to 27 200 in 1987, it starts at 100, rises to 104½ in 1987 and returns to 100. It is saying this: 'For every 100 people over 65 in 1981 there will be between 104 and 105 in 1987, and by 1991 there will again be 100'.

In just the same way, indexed graphs can be produced for each of the three age groups within that total, each of them showing how many people there will be in subsequent years for every 100 in 1981.

Figure 6 goes one stage further: it brings all this information together on a single graph. And what is now vividly exposed is the dramatic increase expected in the over-85s: for every 100 in 1981 there will be no fewer than 161 in 1991. It also reveals very clearly that the total population will stay much the same because there will be far fewer people in the 65-74 age group.

That information was there in Figure 4. It was indexing that brought it out.

2 Rates

Rates may call to your mind those unwelcome bills from your local council, and these are indeed one particular form of the general principle of rating: the council announces a rate of, say, 95p in the pound, and you then know that if your house has a rateable value of £500 you will have to find 500 x 95p = £475.

You have also probably come across birth rates: perhaps there were 2400 births last year in your district containing 200 000 people: in other words, for every 1000 inhabitants there were 12 births, and the birth rate was therefore 12 per 1000.

If a neighbouring district's birth rate was only 11, what can you conclude? Virtually nothing on that information alone, because the characteristics of the two districts may be dissimilar: in particular, your district may contain a higher proportion of women of childbearing age.

Rates that ignore the characteristics of a population are known as crude rates; those that take account of the number of people in each age group are described as age-specific; if they also take account of the number of men and women in the population they are called age and sex-specific.

The next two examples show how current rates were used to predict future levels of activity for planning purposes.

61/Plans and projects

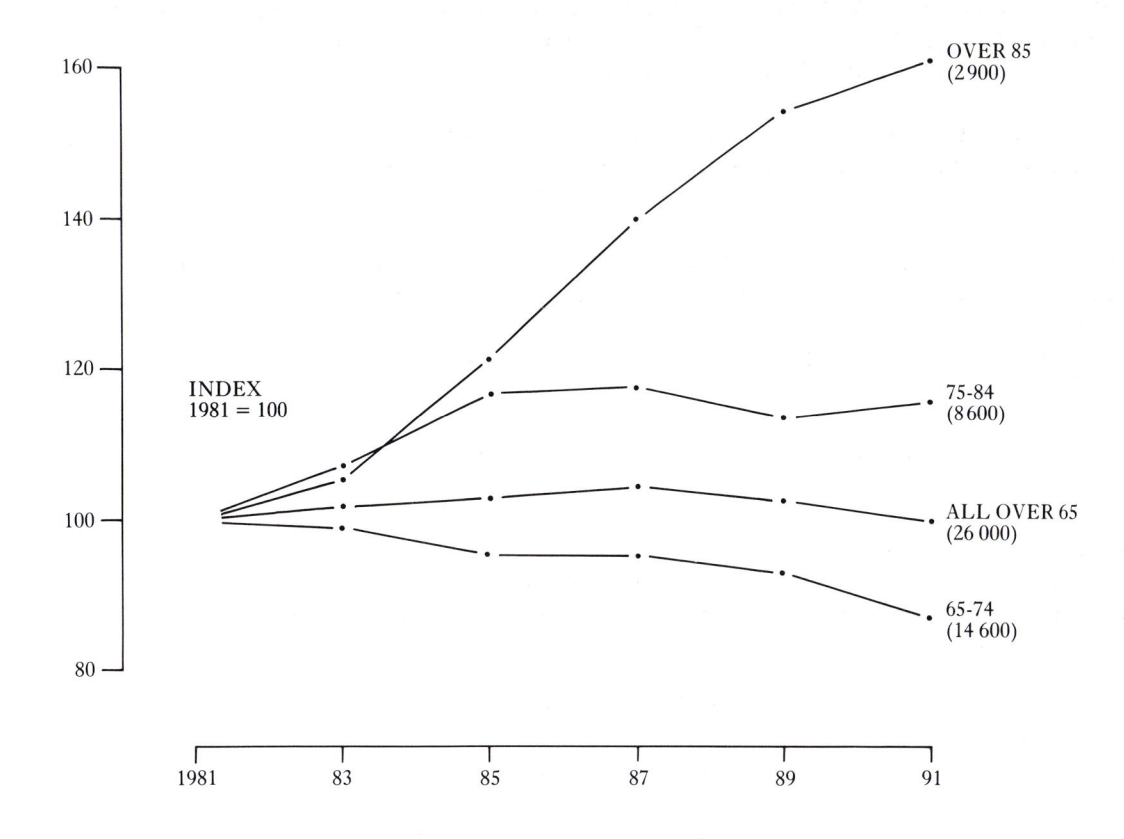

Figure 6 Marchmain Health Authority
       Elderly population by age, 1981-1991 (mid-1991 projections shown in brackets)

SOURCE: COUNTY PLANNING DEPARTMENT

The case of the proliferous visits

In 1981, Marchmain's community nursing staff carried out 400 000 visits to their 200 000 population, a crude rate of 2 visits per person. But over two-thirds of those visits were to people aged over 65, who accounted for only about one-eighth of the district's population (see Table 7, page 62).

62/*From figures to facts*

Table 7 Marchmain Health Authority
Community nursing staff visiting rates, 1981

1	2 1981 Population	3 No of Visits	4 Visiting rate per 100 (col 3 ÷ col 2 ×100)
Age 0– 4	13 000	54 000	415
5–14	33 600	6 000	18
15–64	127 400	70 000	55
65–74	16 800	70 000	417
75–84	7 400	150 000	2027
85+	1 800	50 000	2778

Armed with these visiting rates, Marchmain then applied them to the population they expected to have in their district in 1991 (see Table 8).

Table 8 Marchmain Health Authority
Community nursing staff: projected visits, 1991

1	2 Projected 1991 population	3 Visiting rate per 100, 1981 from Table 7	4 Projected no of visits 1991 (col 2 × col 3 ÷ 100)
Age 0– 4	14 000	415	58 100
6–14	34 000	18	6 120
15–64	126 500	55	69 575
65–74	14 600	417	60 882
75–84	8 600	2027	174 322
85+	2 900	2778	80 562
			449 561

So the authority could see that, if the 1981 visiting patterns were maintained, the community nurses would be carrying out almost 50 000 more visits in 1991, even though the district's total population was likely to change very little.

Of course, such a calculation is no more than a starting point: all sorts of other factors will operate to modify those figures. In general, though, such factors are likely to increase rather than reduce them, given the emphasis on keeping elderly people in the community and on discharging people more quickly from acute hospital beds.

The case of the under-used hospital

Marchmain had another planning problem: with a bed occupancy of about 55 per cent its 24-bed eye hospital was under-used, and the possibility was being considered of closing it and providing a smaller number of ophthalmic beds in two mixed-specialty wards in the general hospital.

The question was raised whether the impending increase in the population of the elderly would increase the occupancy of the eye hospital. Age-specific admission rates were calculated, along with age-specific lengths of stay to produce the figures in Table 9.

Table 9 Marchmain Eye Hospital
Projected age-specific bed occupancy levels, 1991

1	2	3	4	5	6
	Projected 1991 population	Admissions per 1000 population 1981	Projected 1991 admissions	Average length of stay 1981 days	Projected occupancy 1991 (col 4 × col 5) / 365
Age 0–4	14 000	4.5	63	3.1	0.53
5–14	34 000	2.7	92	4.0	1.01
15–64	126 500	1.7	217	8.0	4.76
65–74	14 600	8.8	129	10.0	3.53
75–84	8 600	14.2	122	10.8	3.61
85+	2 900	13.9	40	12.1	1.33
					14.77

Notice particularly how the final column was calculated. The projected admissions were multiplied by the length of stay (to provide *bed days*) and divided by 365 to give a projected actual daily occupancy. This was done for each age group, and the six results were added together to give a total of 14.77 occupied beds per day, which is 61.5 per cent of the 24 available beds.

Thus in this particular case the increase in the proportion of elderly people within a static population seemed likely to increase levels of occupancy by about 12 per cent from 55 per cent to 61.5 per cent on the basis of current admission and occupancy rates.

But again, this is not the end of the matter. Patients may be staying longer in hospital than necessary because there is so little pressure on the beds; population changes may

64/From figures to facts

not occur as forecast (though changes among the elderly can be predicted quite accurately); treatment methods may change, perhaps affecting the number of people who can be treated as well as the time taken to treat them; and medical policies may change, affecting the proportion treated as outpatients, inpatients and day cases, and so on. Looking into the future always involves some measure of crystal ball-gazing; by using statistical information you make the process less of a wild guessing game.

3 Norms

When considering plans you are likely to see references to norms. A norm is usually expressed in the language of rates, as just described, and defines one or other of two figures: a target, or an average. It is not always made clear whether the norm you are considering is one or the other, but the difference is obviously important. A below *average* district may well have something to worry about; a district which has not attained a particular *target* may not be providing an ideal service, but it may well be no worse than most other districts.

The next illustration shows how an authority calculated a norm and how it then made a policy decision not to achieve it.

The case of the old folks' hospital norms

With its population of 26 000 residents aged 65 and over, Marchmain calculated its requirements for hospital beds and day hospital places according to the norms in Table 10, but after very careful consideration the authority agreed not to give a high priority to achieving these norms.

Table 10 Marchmain District
Geriatric hospital bed and day hospital place requirements, based on DHSS norms of provision

	DHSS norm per 1000 population aged 65+	Marchmain District requirement	Current position	Shortfall
Geriatric beds – long stay	5	130 ⎫	105 ⎫	
– acute	3	78 ⎬ 260	60 ⎬ 210	50
– rehabilitation	2	52 ⎭	45 ⎭	
Geriatric day hospital places	2-3	52–78	40	12–38

They reached this decision for a number of reasons, the chief of which was that – thanks to a positive and successful policy of support in the community – there was little pressure for an increased hospital service: in particular, the hospital's general acute beds were not being blocked by elderly patients, and the day hospital rarely had all its existing places filled. The increase in the proportion of very old people was expected to put added pressures on the geriatric unit, but it was considered that these pressures could be absorbed in various ways, without the need for extra facilities.

In coming to this conclusion, the authority took account of all the services available to the elderly people in their district, including particularly those of the county and district councils (which were close to their norms) and the various voluntary and private homes in the district.

As targets – as they usually are, rather than averages – norms must be viewed with caution. The basis on which they come into existence is often quite arbitrary. They may be based on one particular example of a service which has been singled out at one time as being especially noteworthy. They assume that the service that goes with them is of a particular kind – usually active and progressive. They ignore, or make assumptions about, the complementary services provided by other bodies, including local authorities and the voluntary and private sectors. And they are seldom kept up to date: the ones in the illustration, for example, date back to the mid-1950s.

Despite all these objections, however, and provided they are applied sensibly, they represent a convenient yardstick for service planning and provide a useful means of assessing levels of service.

Section 2   Introducing a new system

This section describes how an authority introduced a new statistical system for the medical loan service in its district.

The medical loan service (known also by various other names, such as the nursing equipment loan service) is basically a system for loaning equipment for people to use in their homes. In practice, it extends considerably further than this and can include the loan of furniture as well as equipment; the issue of expendable products, such as incontinence aids, and the laundering of clothing by hospital laundries. It complements (and often overlaps) a similar service provided by local authority social services departments and by some voluntary bodies, particularly the Red Cross and St John's.

In financial terms, the service accounts for only a tiny fraction of health service expenditure; but its value is out of all proportion to its cost as it greatly improves the quality of life, even to the extent of permitting people to lead independent lives in the community instead of having to move into institutional care.

In this particular case the authority recognised the importance of allowing the service to expand; but because the records were maintained manually on a day-to-day basis, it was very difficult to assess how the service was being used, let alone how it could best be developed.

To overcome these problems (and also to allow the service to operate more efficiently) the authority introduced a computerised records system. This produced three kinds of information:

1. operational outputs
2. statistical analyses
3. costing information

This section describes the second of these, the statistical analyses.

The system recorded the following data about the use of the medical loan service within the district:

patients – number and age group
equipment – number and type
waiting – number and length of wait
source of referral
deliveries and collections
patients with equipment on loan over six months.

A straightforward enough little list, you may feel, and you would be quite right. But the quantity of data involved is enormous, and it takes time and application by busy community staff for it to be put into the computer. Once this has been done, however, it is a simple matter to call up any number of analyses: the real skill lies in working out who needs what, and why.

How relevant are the techniques described earlier in the chapter?

Consider *rates*. The data recorded the total number of loans in the first year of use and the age of each patient receiving a loan, thereby enabling age-related loan rates to be calculated (see Table 11).

Table 11 Goodwin Health Authority
Medical loan service age-related loan rates, 1981

Age range	Population 1981	Medical loans	Loans per 1000 population 1981
0–4	15 000	31	2.1
5–15	36 000	383	10.6
16–64	128 000	1547	12.1
65–74	15 500	2477	159.8
75–80	6 200	1990	321.0
80+	4 500	2948	655.0
all ages	205 200	9376	45.7

What did the authority learn from these figures? Clearly, that little use was being made of the service by the under-65s, but that those over that age used the service much more heavily, and the older they became the more use they made of it.

Future changes in the level of use can also be *indexed* to projected population changes (see Figure 7, page 68).

Just how valuable is this graph? Consider how it compares with a straightforward indexed population projection for the district (see Figure 8, page 69).

Because it has been assumed that the equipment will be loaned at the same rates after 1981 as they were in 1981 the shape of the two graphs is exactly the same; only the figures are different, and they need to be looked at with care. The percentage increase in the projected number of children under 5 (29 per cent) is not far short of the over-80s (35 per cent); but the increase in the actual number of loans is 9 and 1041 respectively! Does it really help to index in such circumstances?

You will not find much use for *norms* in a medical loan service, and none exist.

The authority which introduced the system selected several analyses: these helped them to see what sort of service was being provided, how it was being used and who was making use of it. Figures 9-12 (pages 70-73) provide four examples in summarised form.

68/*From figures to facts*   Figure 7   Goodwin Health Authority
Medical loan service: forecast medical loan based on 1981 loan rates and OPCS population projections

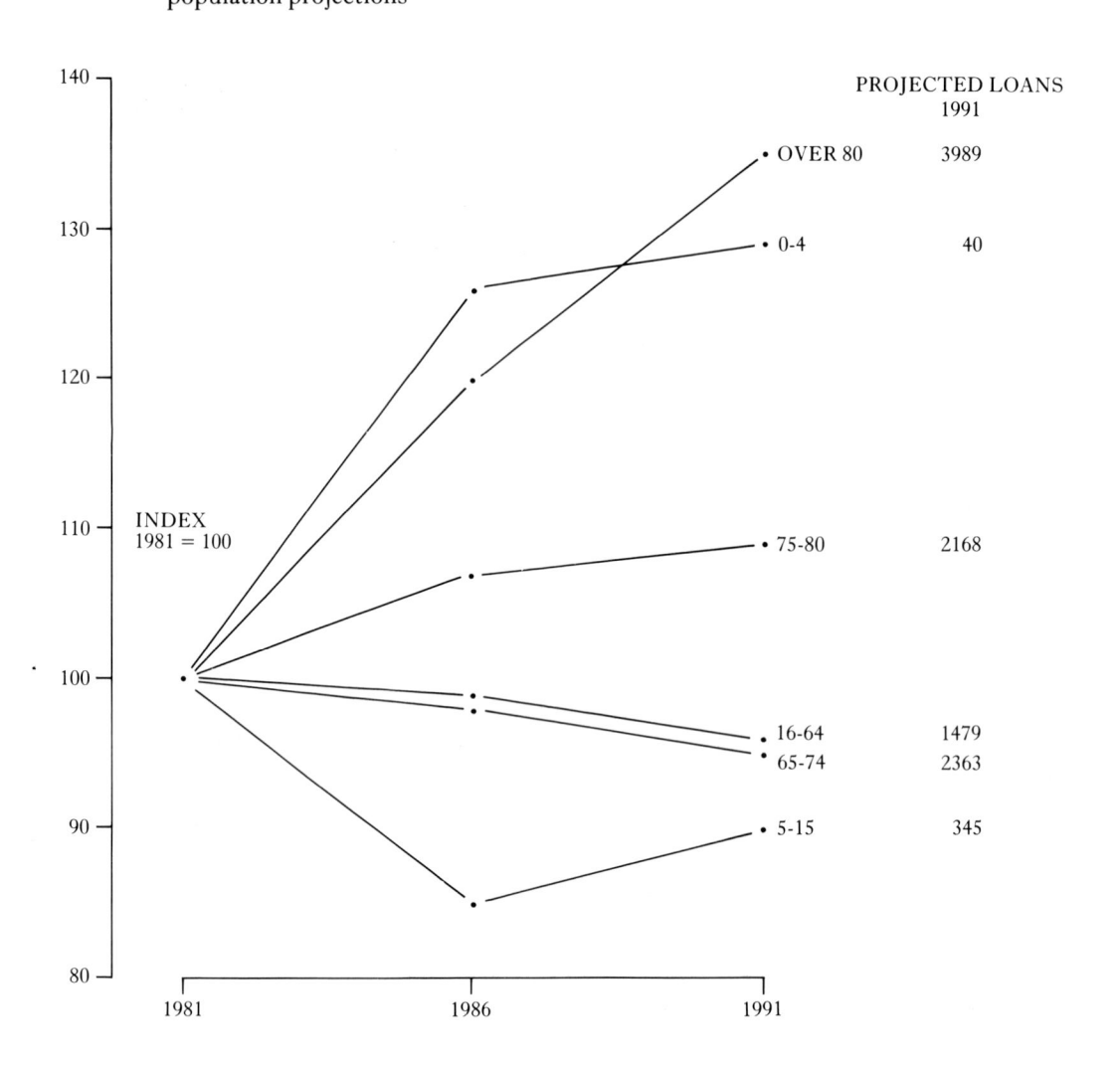

	PROJECTED LOANS 1991
OVER 80	3989
0-4	40
75-80	2168
16-64	1479
65-74	2363
5-15	345

INDEX 1981 = 100

Figure 8 Goodwin Health Authority
District population projections

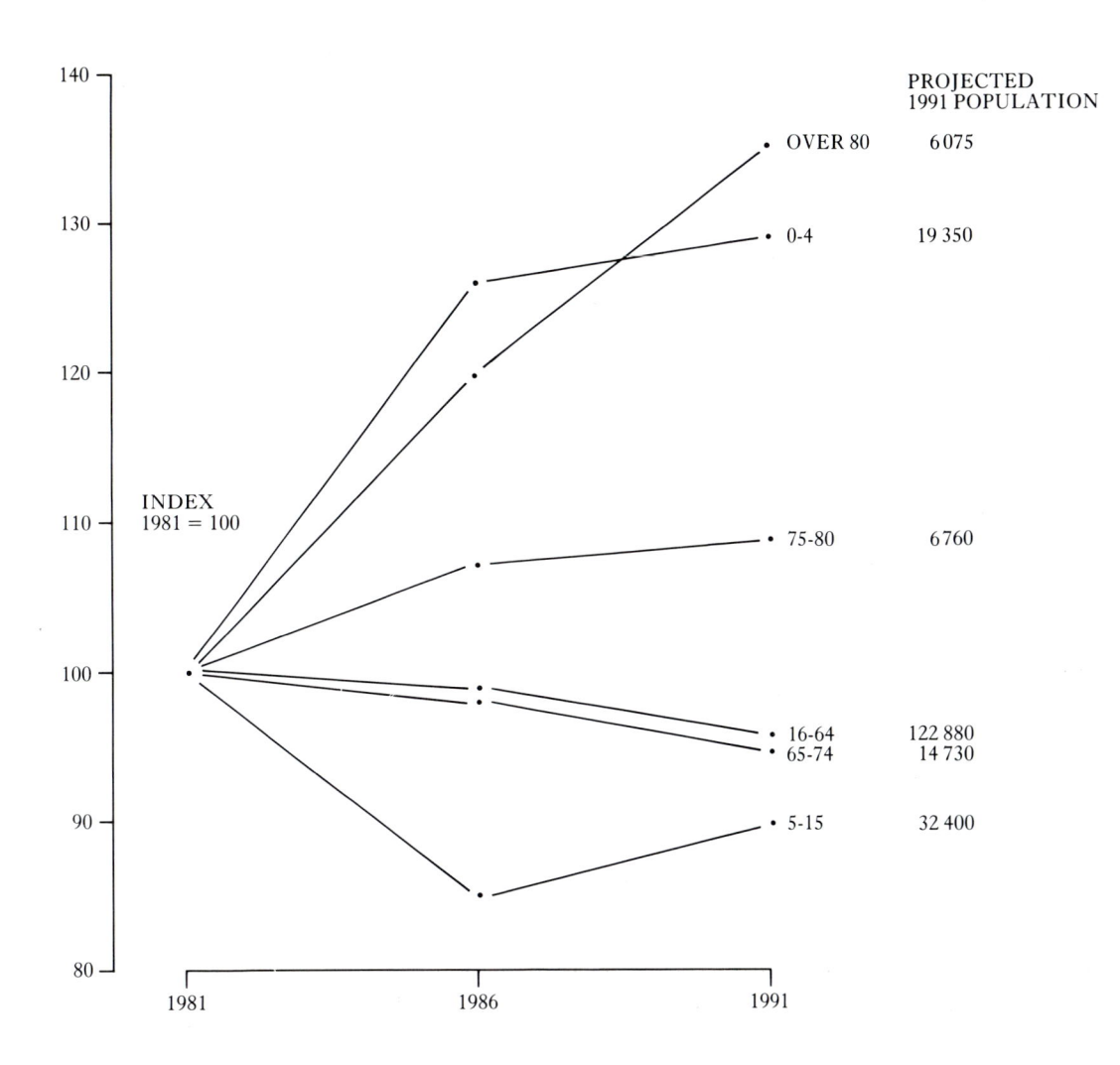

69/Plans and projects

INDEX 1981 = 100

	PROJECTED 1991 POPULATION
OVER 80	6 075
0-4	19 350
75-80	6 760
16-64	122 880
65-74	14 730
5-15	32 400

Figure 9 Equipment on loan and waiting lists, 2 February 1983

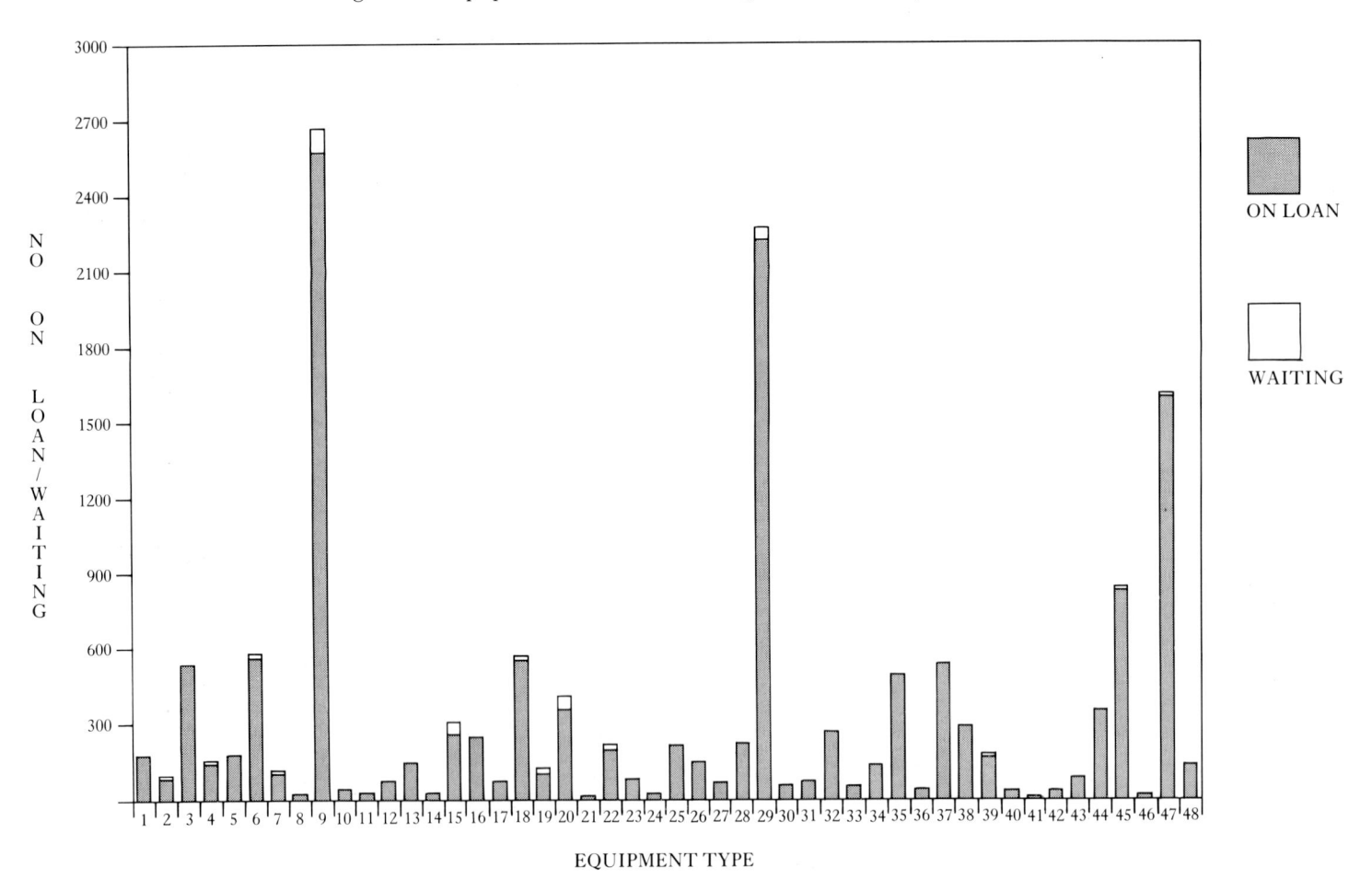

This figure shows, among other things, that four types of equipment are required far more than the others (the key to the table shows that these are commodes, pick-up walkers, wheelchairs and walking sticks); also, that although waiting lists are small in comparison with the various totals, they still amount to several hundred.

Figure 10 Waiting time for four equipment items with longest waiting lists

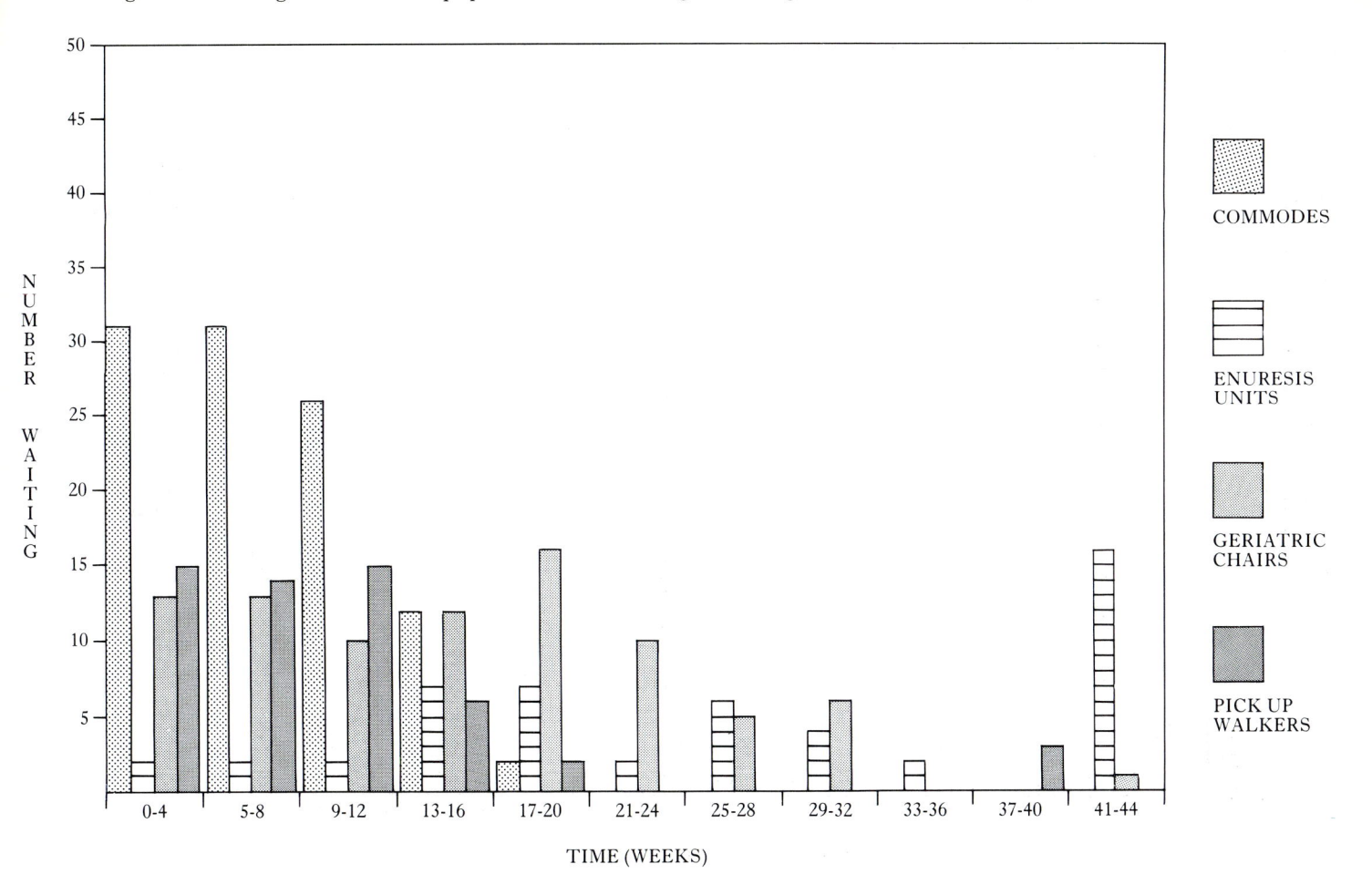

This figure shows, for example, that almost threequarters of the 115 patients needing commodes have been waiting for over a month and that the average wait for an enuresis unit is five or six months.

Figure 11 Number of items on loan per patient, 2 February 1983

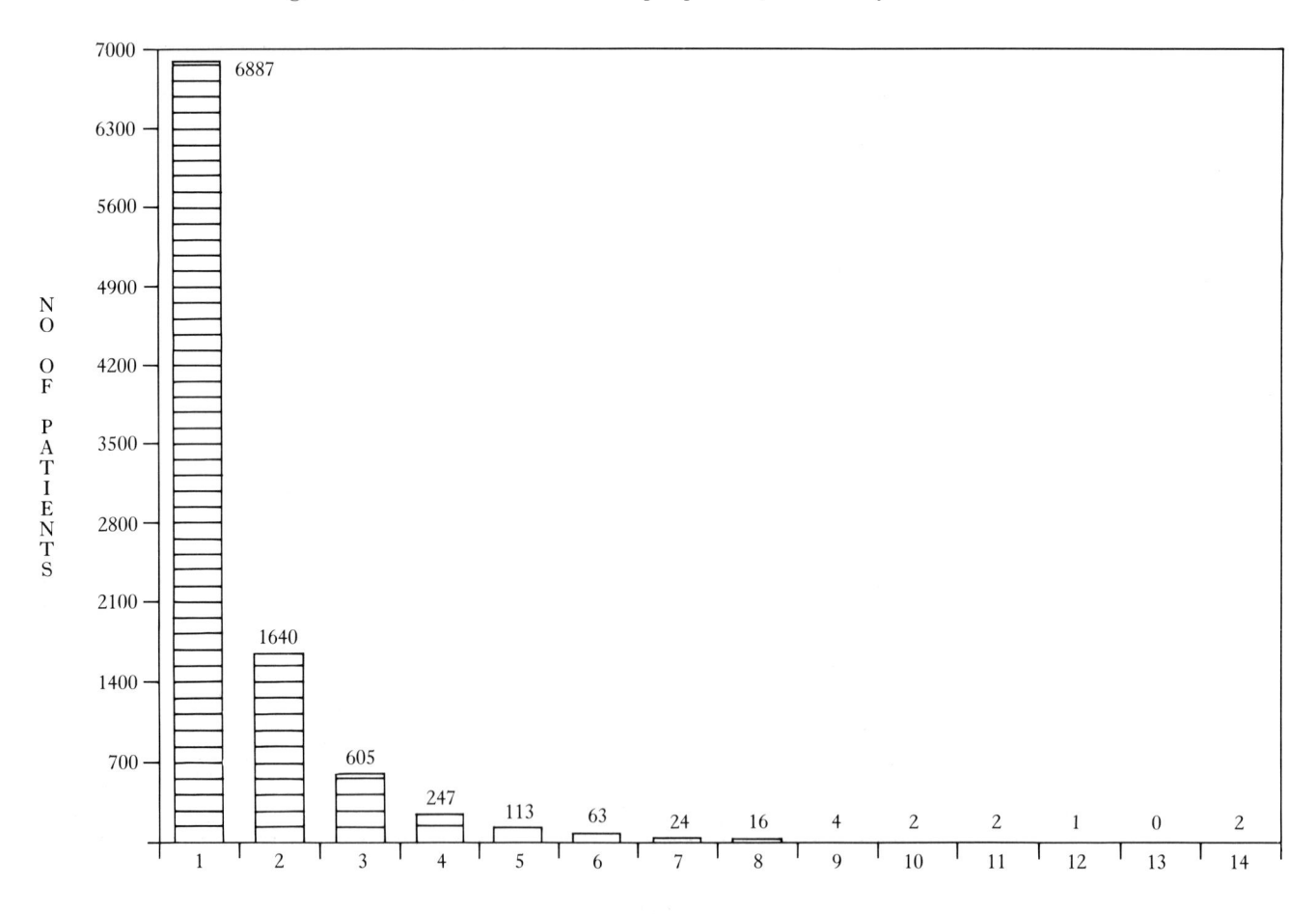

NO OF PATIENTS

Number of equipment items	No of patients
1	6887
2	1640
3	605
4	247
5	113
6	63
7	24
8	16
9	4
10	2
11	2
12	1
13	0
14	2

NUMBER OF EQUIPMENT ITEMS

This figure reveals, for example, that although the great majority (72 per cent) of patients each had only one item on loan, there were 11 patients who between them were borrowing 118 items.

Figure 12 Source of referral by number of items requested, 1 October to 31 December 1983

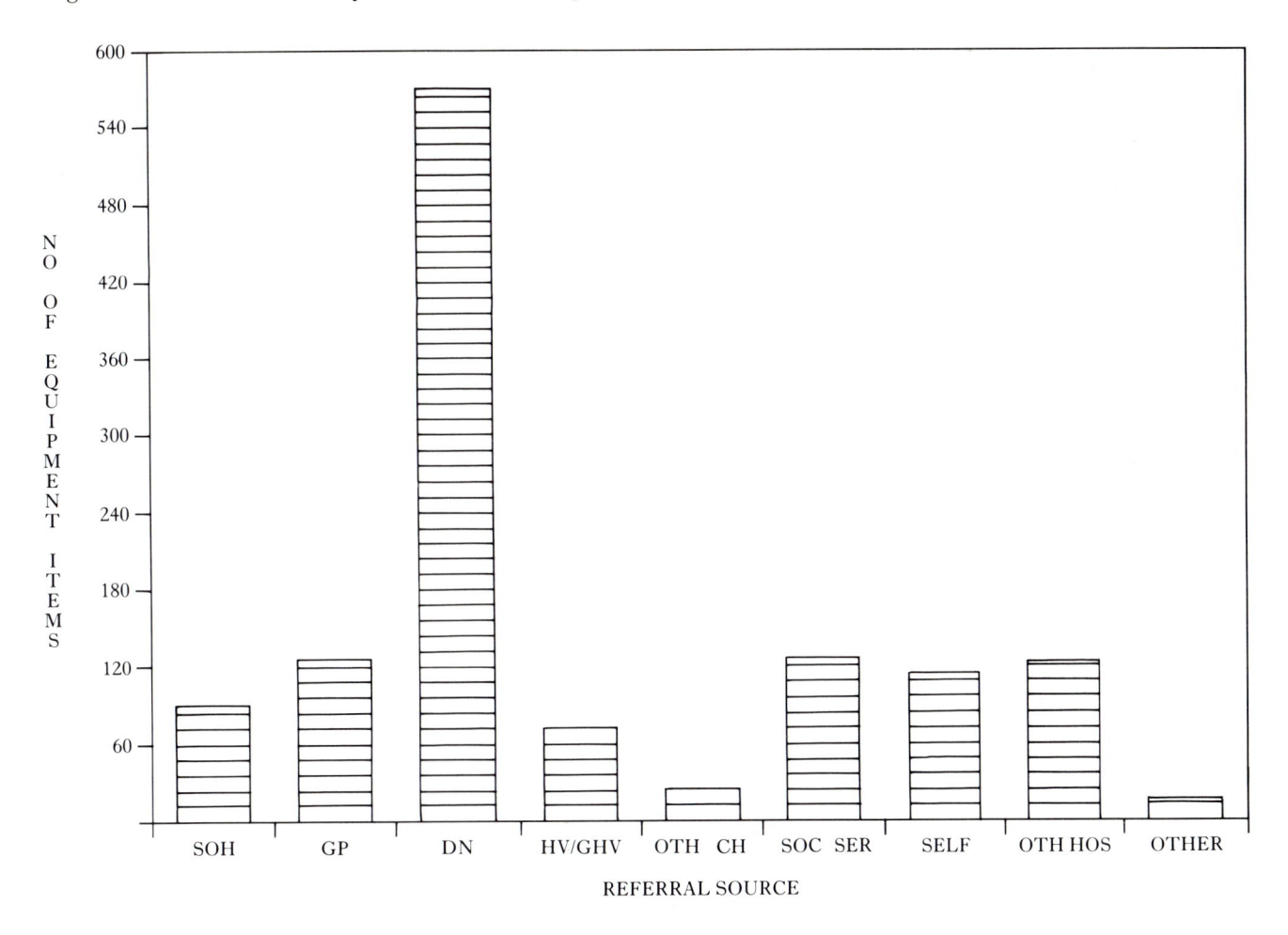

This figure shows, for example, that almost half the requests for equipment are placed by district nurses.

74/From figures to facts Needless to say, these are only a few of the many ways in which the data stored by the computer can be analysed and presented. The authority itself may choose not to receive any information at all about the service unless – exception reporting again! – the broad objectives of providing it are not being met. On the other hand, the staff who are providing and managing it will probably need to know considerably more; and it is up to them to think hard about what they require, for what purpose, in what form, how frequently and for how long – the selfsame basic questions, in other words, as you were being encouraged to consider in Chapter One.

Conclusion

In theory, planning is about anticipating changes in the needs of the population and adjusting services to those changes as they occur.

In practice, it is more often than not about responding: responding to changes in the needs of the population that have *already* occurred; responding to the demands of powerful people within the organisation; responding to external injunctions to do more with less.

Against this background it is more important than ever to base your decisions on accurate, complete and relevant information. This chapter has shown you a few simple ways in which to analyse and present such information so that it can be readily understood.

A vast array of techniques – far beyond the scope of this book – exists for predicting the outcome of the alternative courses of action that may be open to you. If there are staff available to your authority who have the considerable skills involved in operating these techniques you will find them extremely valuable in your aim to make the best possible decisions, and you will probably learn a great deal from them.

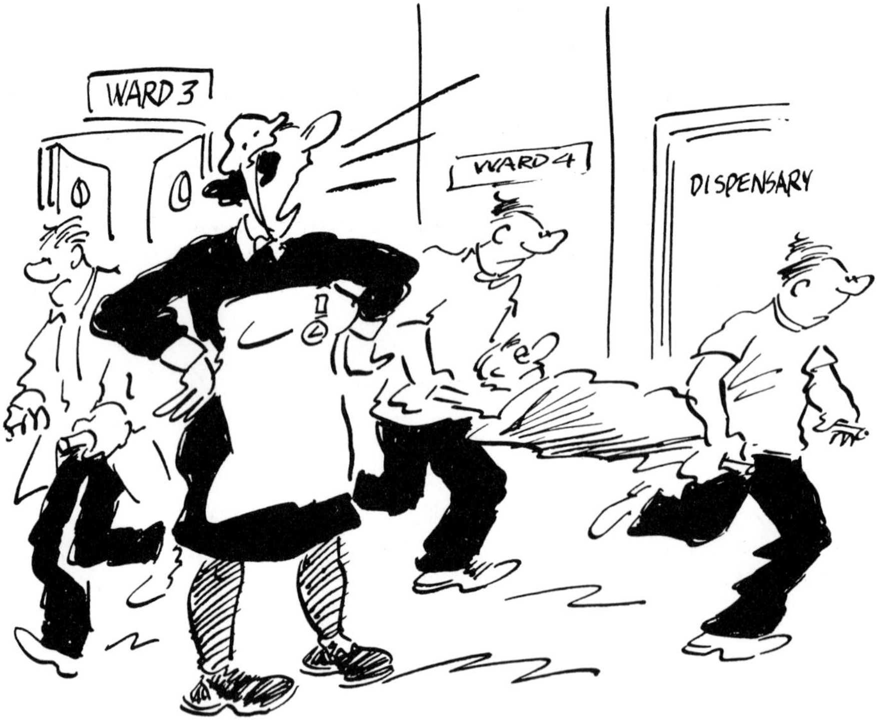
WARD 3
WARD 4
DISPENSARY

CHAPTER FIVE

Manpower control

There is no need to stress the importance of having sound information about staff. Every district in the country has several thousand employees on its books, and staff costs account for some three-quarters of all the money spent on the health service.

This chapter is about a very important part of staff statistics called manpower control. This may conjure up in your mind the sort of picture that you see opposite, and certainly the allocation of staff to their duties is involved, though preferably in a rather less extreme form!

Manpower control covers three particular management responsibilities:

1 *Limiting staff* to agreed numbers (this is called establishment control) or to agreed expenditure costs (financial control), or both;

2 *Making efficient use of staff,* by exercising a careful control over such things as overtime, enhanced payments and when holidays are taken; and by doing everything possible to reduce unnecessary absenteeism and resignations;

3 *Making effective use of staff,* so that the best possible balance is obtained between numbers of patients treated and high standards of care.

You may be wondering about the distinction between efficient and effective. *Efficiency* is borrowed from the meaning given to the term by engineers: an efficient engine is one which uses most of its fuel to make it run. Cars, for example are notoriously inefficient, as less than a third of the energy they consume is used to make them run. *Effectiveness* deals with the ability to achieve a particular objective. As a means of getting people from one place to another, cars are generally effective. It is irrelevant to the question of effectiveness that they do so inefficiently.

Organisations need to be effective in serving the purpose for which they exist. They need also to be efficient if they are to remain competitive, or – in the case of the health service – if they are to remain able to respond to ever-increasing demands.

This chapter describes a familiar situation, with some of the details taken from an actual case, to show how each of these three aspects of manpower control operates.

MARSTAM HEALTH AUTHORITY
Oakridge Hospital, Orthopaedic Unit
Report from the District Management Team

Admissions to the Orthopaedic Unit have risen by almost a third, from 1300 in 1981 to 1725 in 1983, without any increase in the establishment of 20 whole-time equivalent nursing staff (excluding night staff) allocated to the unit.

The District Nursing Officer considers that the pressures on the staff are now so intense that unless additional nurses are appointed, beds will have to be closed. The orthopaedic surgeons agree that more nursing staff are urgently needed; they are insistent, however, that beds should in no circumstances be closed, pointing out that the waiting list exceeds 600, almost half of whom have already been waiting in excess of 12 months.

Although the establishment of the unit has not been exceeded, the nursing allocation is nevertheless overspent, and no funds exist in the District to permit additional nurses to be employed.

The DMT may have no option but to recommend the closure of eight beds on a temporary basis. Before taking this step, however, it has instructed the district personnel and information officers to examine whether this extremely undesirable step can in any way be avoided.

A further report will be made to the authority shortly.

Comment

79/Manpower control

Problems of the sort illustrated opposite have become increasingly common in the health service, and will continue to do so.

Demand rises as the number of elderly people in the population increases and treatments are developed for conditions which previously could not be treated; and this greater demand is matched by more rapid and accurate diagnostic procedures, improved treatment techniques, more effective drugs and more hospital doctors.

But the total number of other staff – unlike that of most hospital doctors – is controlled by district health authorities, who in turn are restricted by the funds they receive. These funds take virtually no account of the increased number of patients treated, and the stresses described in this report are the inevitable result.

This chapter discusses the problems of manpower control in the three sections described initially:

1 Limiting staff
2 Making *efficient* use of staff
3 Making *effective* use of staff

1 Limiting staff

In the first paragraph the report refers to the unit as having an establishment of 20 whole-time equivalent nursing staff. By 'establishment' is meant the number of staff who may be employed in the unit, usually by grade or qualification (sister, staff nurse, enrolled nurse and so on); by 'whole-time equivalent' is meant full-time and part-time staff whose hours of work amount to those worked by 20 full-time nurses: as a full-time nurse works 37½ hours per week the unit may employ nurses within a total of 20 × 37½ = 750 hours per week.

It may surprise you that the nursing allocation had been overspent even though the number of nurses had been kept within this limit. In fact it is quite possible for staff to cost more than the amount allocated without exceeding the establishment. Here are some of the reasons:

1 There are various fixed costs relating to the employment of every member of staff, whether full-time or part-time. In this case it had been assumed that 17 staff would be

full-time and six part-time, a total of 23. In fact, 15 were full-time and 11 part-time, a total of 26. These three extra staff had caused a slight increase in costs compared with the estimate.

2 Nursing staff receive a salary increase in each of the first few years they hold a particular grade. For estimating purposes it is often assumed that staff will on average be paid at the central point of their salary scale. In this case, however, most of the staff had worked on the same grade for several years and were being paid on average very nearly the maximum of their salary scale.

3 There is a tendency for grades to 'drift' upwards either in response to recruitment difficulties or because the work requires higher levels of skill. In this case two enrolled nurses had left and had been replaced by staff nurses, but no increase had been made in the budget to allow for this.

4 Allowances are normally made for overtime working and temporary staff to cover absences, but these may prove inadequate, particularly if sickness rates are unexpectedly high. As you will see later, this proved to be a significant factor in this case.

5 Budgets are sometimes trimmed by one or two per cent on the assumption that posts will not be fully occupied throughout the year; and sometimes authorities are forced to make arbitrary cuts because of unexpected pressures on their allocations.

6 Agreements may be negotiated centrally which increase the payments made to staff, but no extra funds may be allocated to cover these payments.

All this is enough to demonstrate that there is no comfortably precise relationship between the number of staff employed and the cost of employing them.

Individual managers normally use establishments as their primary way of exercising this aspect of manpower control: they seldom possess the expertise, time and computer power to operate from financial controls alone. But as an authority member you have two reasons for concentrating on staff costs, rather than numbers: first, authorities have placed on them an overriding requirement not to overspend; and second, it is incredibly difficult to know at any one time exactly how many staff are employed by the authority. Over and over again, systems for calculating staff numbers have been devised, refined, amended, revised and abandoned. It is to be hoped that the Körner proposals will succeed where so many have failed.

2   Making efficient use of staff

Staff should of course be rewarded properly for the skills they bring to their work, the responsibilities they bear and the disruptions that are so often part and parcel of health service life.

Efficient use is made of staff when these factors are appropriately recognised, the work gets done and no more is spent than is necessary in the process.

Unnecessary expenditure can occur in two ways:

A   From making payments that are not necessary;

B   From losing the services of staff.

A   *Unnecessary payments*

Staff may receive any number of payments over and above their basic pay. Many of these are common enough outside the health service, such as overtime (at various rates), shift and split duty allowances, incentive bonus schemes and payments for working unsocial hours. Others are less common outside the service, like those for working with particular types of patients, being available to return to work if required, operating certain types of equipment, using a private car for health service purposes and so on.

Many of these payments are inseparable from the nature of the health service, with its day and night, seven days per week commitments.

Some are built into systems of working that are so complex, involving a multiplicity of interrelated payments, that special studies are required to unravel them: ambulance services and hospital laundries are typical of such systems and are the happy hunting grounds of management audit specialists, work study engineers and the like. Cost comparisons do exist on a national basis for these two services in particular, and a health authority receiving them will find in them a useful means of comparing the efficiency of its ambulance and laundry services.

But measures of efficiency do not have to be complex. Consider overtime: as it usually involves paying more than the rate for the job, overtime is an indicator of possible inefficiency. Some of it may be unavoidable; but some may go back to the days of full employment, when overtime had to be offered as the only means of attracting staff.

In the orthopaedic unit described, overtime was calculated as a proportion of the 750

82/From figures to facts

nursing hours allowed for in the unit's establishment, and a graph was produced (see Figure 13). The upward trend is unmistakeable; for its cause, read on.

B *Losing the services of staff*
The services of staff may be lost temporarily, when the staff are on holiday or study leave (which can be planned and allowed for) or when they are sick (which cannot); or they may be lost permanently, when they resign.

Both sickness and resignations raise important questions of efficiency. Staff are (very properly) paid their salary when they are sick, but their work still has to be done, and very often this involves paying overtime to other staff or taking on temporary staff. When someone leaves, the work must still be done while the post is empty, often at a cost greater than the salary of the person who has left; and the new employee usually takes time to settle in before contributing fully to the work of the unit.

In the orthopaedic unit described, *sickness* rates were found to be a major factor. They had doubled in the previous two years and accounted entirely for the increased overtime, as well as for the employment of agency nurses from time to time.

Sickness rates are normally calculated as a percentage of normal working hours: thus, if one person is sick in a department employing 20 staff, the sickness rate is one-twentieth, that is, 5 per cent.

In the case of the unit described, the sickness rate was compared with the other units and wards in the hospital (Figure 14). The comparison was shown on a distribution chart:

Figure 13 Oakridge Hospital Orthopaedic Unit
          Hours of overtime paid and worked, quarters June 1981 to March 1983

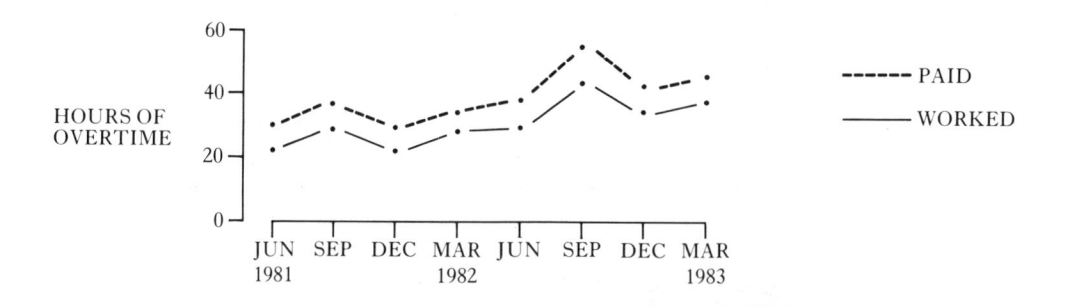

the various rates appear along the bottom of the graph, and the height of the bars above each rate indicates the number of wards having that rate.

So the orthopaedic unit's sickness rate was amongst the four highest rates in the hospital and over double the general level; and, at 10 per cent, it meant that on average there were two nursing staff unable to contribute to the work of the unit throughout the whole of those three months.

High sickness rates are often related to stress at work, a complex subject outside the scope of this book. Suffice it to say that sympathetic management action was applied and the unit's sickness rate was halved.

In the language of manpower control, *resignations* are expressed in terms of turnover rates: if ten people resign in a year in a department of 20 people, the rate of turnover is 50 per cent. Of course, this does not tell you how many *posts* have been involved: it could be that one post amongst the 20 is so unattractive that all ten resignations have been from that one post.

In the case of the orthopaedic unit the turnover rate was found to be low, and no further action was required.

Figure 14 Oakridge Hospital
Sickness rates, June quarter 1983

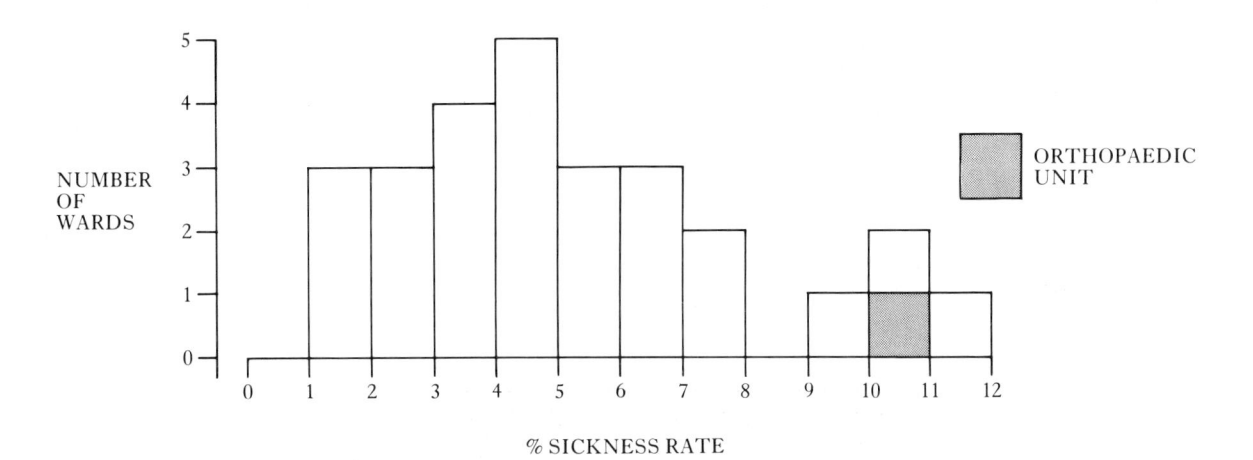

Authorities are seldom told anything about staff sickness and turnover rates in their districts. But these rates can be important, pointing to possible stresses within the organisation. You would be making a valuable contribution to the efficiency of your district by ensuring that these rates are reviewed and acted upon by managers and by considering whether the highest rates should be reported to the authority.

You should not conclude, however, that when you have examined sickness and turnover rates you have exhausted the scope for efficiency, as this particular authority discovered.

It was found that the nursing staff's half-hour morning break had been extended from 30 to 40 minutes. This was to take account of the distance nurses had to walk for their refreshments, and the extra ten minutes were counted as part of their hours of duty. Ten minutes may not seem very much, but they were being taken at the busiest time of the day. Arrangements were made for the refreshments to be brought to the unit, and three hours per week of valuable nursing time were restored.

3   Making effective use of staff

It is a fair generalisation that the more staff there are in a unit, the higher the quality of care but the greater the cost, and vice versa. The aspect of manpower control that considers the effective use of staff is in the business of striking a balance between quality and cost.

You may believe that after all these years there must be plenty of yardsticks which you can use to decide how many staff there should be to a ward or department, according to its workload. In fact, there are very few, and those that do exist are regarded with suspicion at best, derision at worst.

It is not that the question has been ignored: far from it. It is simply that there are so many variables that what may be just right for one situation may be quite inadequate for another and excessive for another, even though on the face of it they seem just the same. On a hospital ward, for example, the need for nursing time and skills will vary according to the nature of the work, the dependency of the patients, personal views of the medical staff about the intensity and frequency of nursing attention, the availability of supporting staff, the type of equipment being used, and so on.

Yardsticks bring problems of their own: units that exceed them expend time and energy justifying why they do so; and those that fall short of them battle for the resources needed to attain them.

Straight comparisons between similar units bring with them a further complicating factor.

There is no uniform way of calculating staff numbers. Two units may perhaps appear to have the same number of staff; but in reality they may be entirely different, simply because in one of them overtime and temporary staff are added in, but in the other they are not.

But there is a growing impetus for standardising statistics, and before very long it will be possible for authorities to make comparisons, confident that like is being compared with like.

In the meantime, what can be done?

Consider the report on the unit again: admissions up by a third, no increase in nursing staff.

Does this mean that there were a third more patients in the unit? This may well be implied, but in fact the patients were being sent home a lot sooner. As a result the occupancy level had risen by only about one-eighth (Figure 15). Of course, the nurses' workload had increased more than this, because the patients were in general more dependent.

You may feel that these figures do at least demonstrate that the number of nurses on the

Figure 15 Marstam District Orthopaedic Unit
Admissions and bed occupancy, 1981-1983 (1983 figures in brackets)

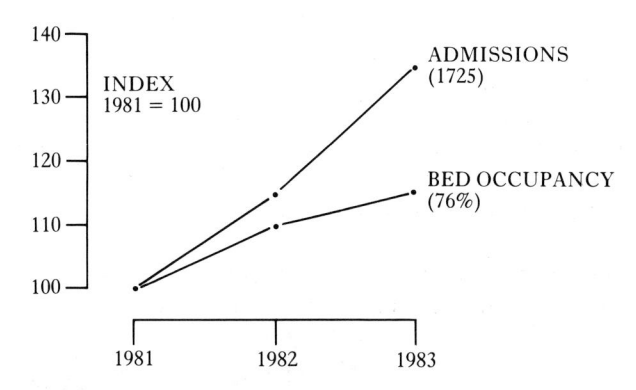

unit should be increased by somewhere between an eighth and a third. But in arriving at this conclusion you have made an assumption: that the level was correct two years ago. And as you have seen, there is simply no way of proving – or disproving – that, just as there is no way of proving or disproving that the present level is too low.

So what happened next?

With no yardsticks to go by or national or regional comparisons to make, the authority decided it would try to make a comparison within its own boundaries.

An analysis was made over three months of the number of patients in every acute ward in the district, and this was related to the number of day-time hours of nursing time provided in each ward in that period. A distribution chart was then prepared (Figure 16).

This chart showed that the orthopaedic unit appeared to have fewer nursing hours available to each of its patients than every other ward. Crude though the calculation was, it provided the nurse managers with a useful starting point for an examination of staffing levels; and as a result, the unit's staffing level was increased by two by means of reallocations within the district's total establishment.

Figure 16 Marstam District Acute Wards
Available nursing hours per patient, June quarter 1983

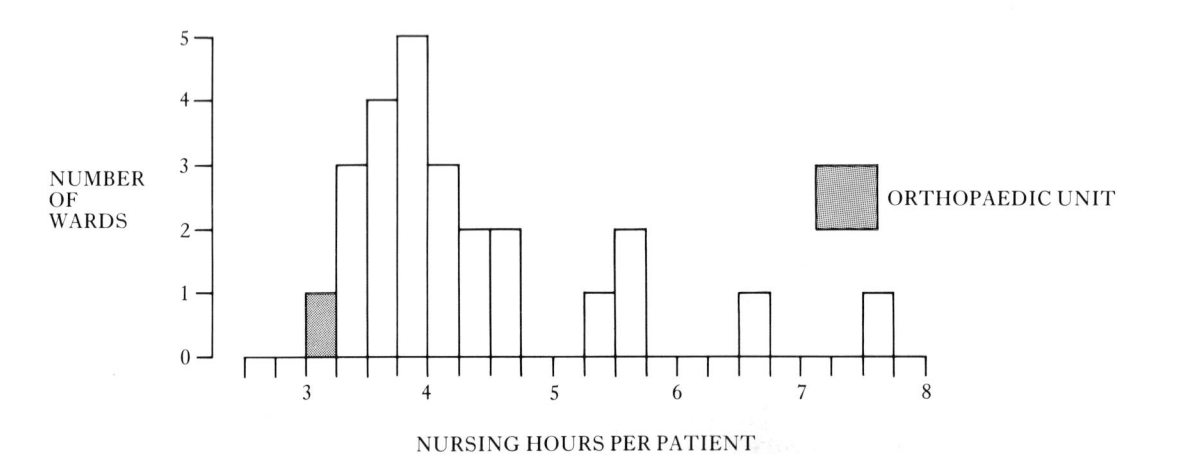

Conclusion

As a result of nothing more than a careful analysis of its manpower statistics, followed by appropriate management action, this district was able both to avoid the closure of badly needed beds and to bring a substantially higher workload within the capacity of the staff concerned. Nothing magical was done, nor was a high level of expertise involved.

Manpower control is in its infancy in the health service, but the picture is changing rapidly.

One of the most important changes will be a far greater ability to relate inputs to outputs – in this case, staff employed to patients treated – in a far less rough and ready way than at present. The prospect of further improvements in analytical techniques, however, should not stop authorities from making sensible use of existing techniques, as this chapter has demonstrated.

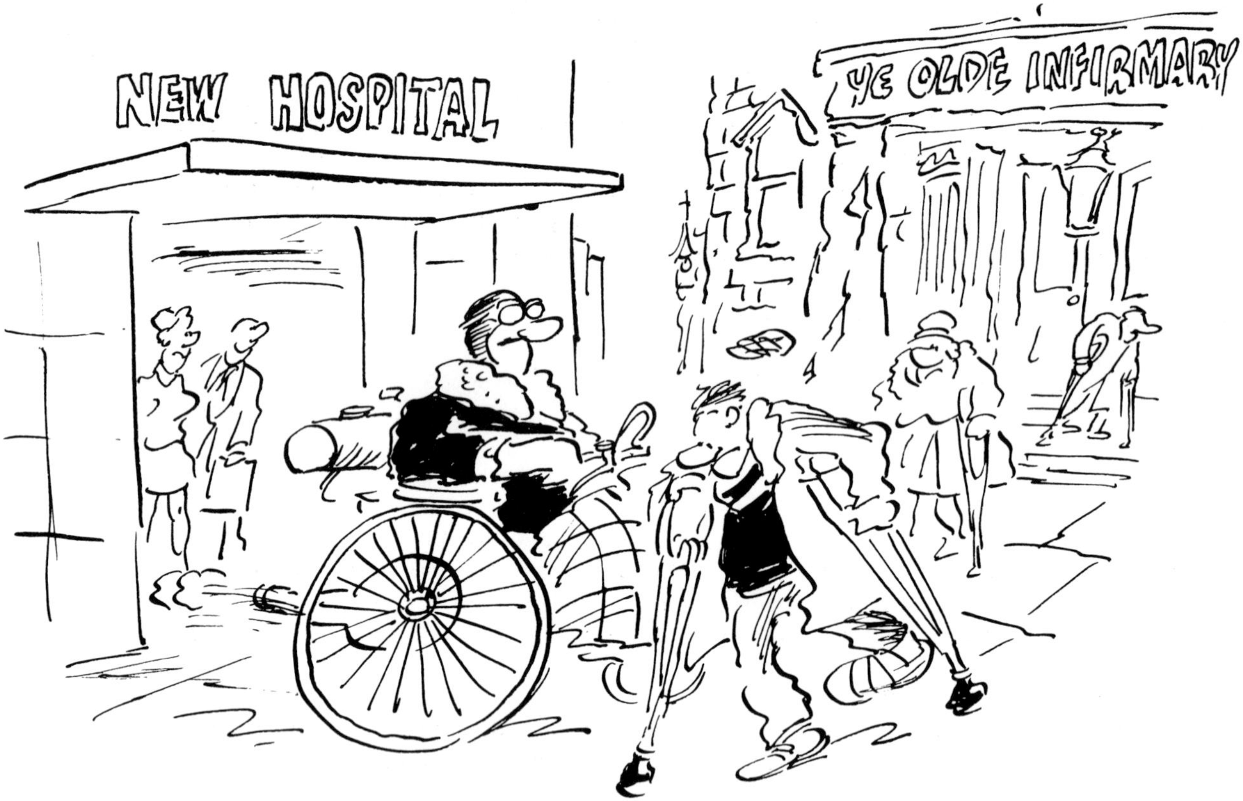
NEW HOSPITAL
YE OLDE INFIRMARY

CHAPTER SIX

Comparisons between districts

When you visit a hospital regularly you soon get to know many of the staff – by sight, if not by name – and the patients too, if it is a long-stay hospital. Before long you find yourself making judgments about the hospital based on your observations and conversations and, although you realise that you cannot assess technical matters like the appropriateness and effectiveness of the treatment the patients are receiving, you may feel that you at least have a fairly good idea about the general atmosphere of the place.

Unfortunately, you could be completely wrong.

A few years ago a caring and conscientious chairman had to admit to a formal enquiry that he had visited a hospital and found nothing untoward only days before a major crisis had broken out.

This chapter is about a recent technique which authorities and their staff are using more and more to check their own impressions about the quality of the service provided in their hospitals. Developed by John Yates of Birmingham University's Health Services Management Centre, this technique uses freely available statistics to define where a district's service stands in relation to all the other districts in England which provide that service.

The statistics have all been around, scattered and little used, for many years. What is new and original is the assembly, analysis and presentation of the figures in such a way that the messages they contain come across rapidly and vividly.

Some aspects of the technique have recently been copied by the Department of Health and Social Security, and you may have heard references – not always wildly enthusiastic – to 'performance indicators' (an expression coined by John Yates and adopted by the DHSS for their analyses). It is important not to confuse the two: the DHSS's figures are at present largely tentative and untried; those of John Yates have been refined over several years, and their reliability in indicating performance failure has been demonstrated repeatedly. Hospitals that have been subjected to special enquiries, for example, and those at which staff have been prosecuted for offences against patients, have almost all tended to have three or more indicators of poor performance in their profiles.

The illustration

The chairman's report that follows is semi-fictitious in order to conceal identities. It is not so unreal however as to prevent a chill from coursing through the nervous systems of many members and senior staff, who have seen similar reports as a last-ditch warning of impending catastrophe. In this case the chairman's recommendations were approved, and the crisis was averted. If performance indicators had already been in use in the district there could well have been no crisis to avert.

Confidential

THRIPTON HEALTH AUTHORITY
St Sebastian's Hospital
Report from the Chairman

On 2 June last I received a request for a private meeting from three members of the staff of St Sebastian's Hospital. In accordance with my normal practice I asked them to confirm that they had taken up the matter with their appropriate heads of department or to state why they considered it inappropriate to do so. They replied that they had talked to their heads of department who had expressed the view that as the matter did not relate to their departments they did not wish to take it up. I accordingly agreed to meet them.

At the meeting they expressed concern about the attitudes and general morale of the nursing staff. They had all worked in mental handicap hospitals prior to coming to St Sebastian's and were in no doubt that the nurses at those hospitals were kinder towards the patients and generally gave them more support and encouragement than at St Sebastian's. Whilst they had not seen any instances of deliberate cruelty at St Sebastian's they felt that the impatience of the staff and their occasionally aggressive behaviour were signs that they were under considerable stress.

I was impressed by the sincerity of the staff at this meeting. They were prepared if necessary to give evidence to a formal enquiry; on the other hand they felt that such an enquiry would be counter-productive, as it would probably create resentment and harden attitudes. They readily accepted however that I would need to report their anxieties to the authority and discuss them with senior managers.

I have had a preliminary meeting with the District Nursing Officer and the Director of Nursing Services for the Mental Handicap Unit. They accept that the nurse staffing levels are lower than they would like but have told me that between 1970 and 1981 the ratio of staff to patients has almost doubled, from 30 nurses per hundred in 1970 to 56 in 1981. The year-on-year figures at the end of my report confirm this (Figure 17).

I have also discussed the situation with the DMT and on the basis of all my discussions I should like to propose action on the following lines:

1. That the authority invite the Development Team for the Mentally Handicapped to pay a further visit to the district. It is now three years since their last visit, and it would be very helpful for the Authority to have a view from this independent source about standards in the district generally and at St Sebastian's.

2. That the Authority take up membership of the British Institute of Mental Handicap at a cost of £150 pa and encourage staff of all disciplines to attend its courses and seminars, as appropriate. It is widely accepted that frequent contact with fellow professionals at activities of this sort constitutes an important means of raising standards.

3. That the authority seek information from the Health Services Management Centre, University of Birmingham about the performance of St Sebastian's Hospital compared with other mental handicap hospitals. The technique employed by the Centre was described at a seminar of authority chairmen which I attended at Stratford upon Avon recently, and I believe that we can obtain valuable information from this source.

Figure 17 St Sebastian's Hospital
Nursing staff:patient ratios, 1970-1982

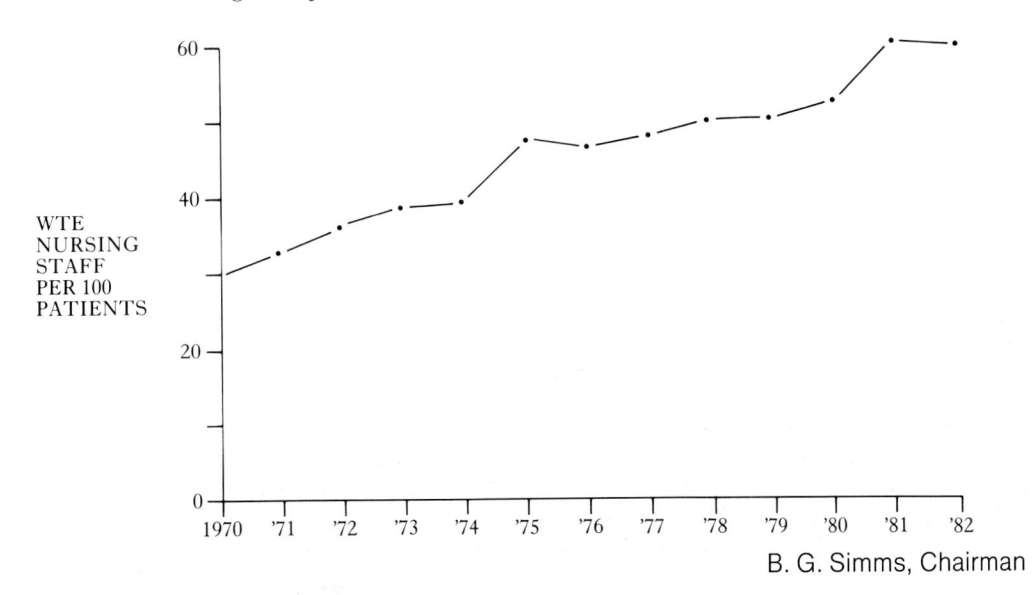

B. G. Simms, Chairman

92/*From figures to facts* The authority accepted all the chairman's proposals, and where Proposal 3 was concerned, they obtained the following information from the Health Services Management Centre:

1 A *profile* of St Sebastian's Hospital;

2 A set of *histograms* showing the position of St Sebastian's in relation to all the other mental handicap hospitals in England;

3 A *historical profile* of the hospital, showing relative performance over time;

along with an explanation of the method and observations on aspects of the information which appeared to the Centre to warrant comment.

1 The profile

Take a careful look at Figure 18, the profile for St Sebastian's Hospital. You will see that down the left-hand side there are six indicators and on the right there are six long rectangles called percentile bars. Between them there are two columns of figures: the

Figure 18 Mental handicap hospitals' profile (for 1982)

INDICATOR	RANGE FOR ALL HOSPITALS	FIGURE FOR ST SEBASTIANS	POSITION RELATIVE TO OTHER HOSPITALS (EXPRESSED AS A PERCENTILE)
SIZE OF HOSPITAL	63-1299	263	☆ (≈60)
PATIENTS PER CONSULTANT	74.3-4054.6	360.3	☆ (≈70)
PATIENTS PER NURSE	0.70-2.85	1.81	☆ (≈90)
PATIENTS PER THERAPIST	6.0-464	21.8	☆ (≈55)
PATIENTS PER PSYCHOLOGIST	40-4966	442	☆ (≈60)
LENGTH OF STAY	79-6499	5742	☆ (≈95)

We incorporate changes to our data base whenever errors are pointed out. Errors in one hospital's data not only alter the figures for that hospital, but can make a small change in the relative position of a number of other hospitals. It is, however, very unusual for data errors to make significant changes to this diagram.

Explanation of method of calculation and list of further indicators available.

range for all the 100 hospitals included in the survey, and the particular figure for St Sebastian's Hospital.

93/Comparisons between districts

What does it mean?

Take the first line, 'size of hospital'. The 'range' column shows that the 98 hospitals ranged in size from 63 to 1299 beds, and the next column shows that St Sebastian's had 263 beds. The star exactly in the centre of the percentile bar indicates that exactly half the hospitals in the survey had fewer beds than St Sebastian's and half had more.

Notice that this is not the same as saying that St Sebastian's had the same number of beds as the national average: it might have, it might not. The profile is interested in showing only how many hospitals had fewer beds than St Sebastian's and how many had more.

The second line shows the number of patients to each consultant, ranging from about 74 at best to over 4000 at worst, with St Sebastian's at 360. This time the star in the adjacent rectangle appears close to 60, showing that some 60 per cent of hospitals had a better ratio of patients to consultants than St Sebastian's.

In just the same way, line 3 shows that over 85 per cent of the hospitals had fewer patients per nurse than 1.81, the ratio at St Sebastian's. If you find it difficult to visualise 1.81 patients, why not think of it as 181 patients for every 100 nurses?

The next two lines show a better position for both therapists and psychologists, but the final line shows that virtually every hospital in England had achieved a shorter length of stay than St Sebastian's at 5742 days. Notice the huge range, 79-6499 days: under three months to almost 18 years. No wonder St Sebastian's shows up as being none too wonderful with its average of one discharge per bed every 15½ years!

So this is the standard profile for mental handicap hospitals: six indicators. Various additional indicators are obtainable on request. The important thing to notice is this: the closer the indicator is to the left-hand edge of the bar the better its performance relative to other hospitals. As it moves to the right it worsens, and every star appearing in the right-hand box means that the hospital concerned is amongst the poorest 15 per cent in the country.

Of course, that is not the end of the story: there may be good reasons for the hospital to be there and to remain there. The term 'indicator' is carefully chosen: just as a car is not necessarily going to change direction when its indicator flashes, so there is not

Figure 19 Inter-hospital comparisons for mental handicap, 1982

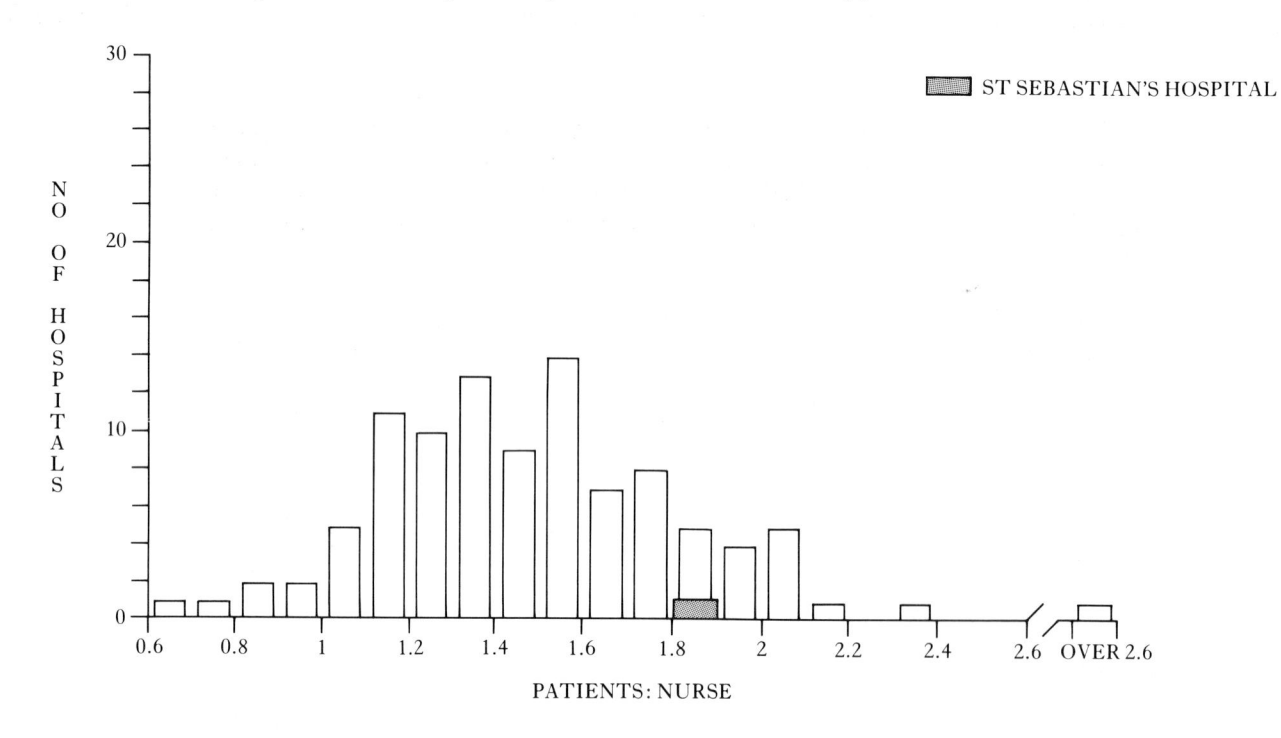

▧ ST SEBASTIAN'S HOSPITAL

NO OF HOSPITALS

PATIENTS: NURSE

100 MENTAL HANDICAP HOSPITALS FOR 1982

PATIENTS PER NURSE

Indicates: The amount of nursing time devoted to the care of inpatients.

Value judgements: A very high number of patients per nurse might make care difficult.

Reservations: 1. Different groups of patients will have different dependency levels, and if staffing is adjusted to take acoount of this, the indicator could be misleading. In practice some hospitals which have a large proportion of high dependency patients are also very badly staffed. This situation may have arisen because this type of work makes staff recruitment much more difficult.
2. A crude patient to nurse ratio takes no account of the mix of nursing skills.
3. The two census dates, themselves three months apart, may not be typical of the year's workload.
4. Nursing workload not undertaken on the wards cannot be separated from the total, which might make its association with the number of inpatients suspect.

Method of calculation: The number of inpatients (31 December) divided by the total number of nurses expressed as a whole time equivalent at 30 September and as recorded on form SBH112.

John Yates   17 November 1983

necessarily anything of concern in a hospital when the indicator puts it at the right-hand end of the percentile bar: but you would be unwise to ignore it!

2 Histogram

For each indicator in the profile there is a chart giving a breakdown of the hospitals within the range. It is called a histogram, a word that simply describes a chart consisting of a series of vertical bars. It is also called a frequency diagram or frequency distribution chart, though there is no need to remember either term: all that matters is to know how to make sense of it.

Look at Figure 19. This is the histogram for the third line in Figure 18, 'patients per nurse'. The top of the tallest bar is level with the figure 14 in the column labelled 'number of hospitals'. It stands just to the left of the 1.6 on the line marked 'patients: nurse'. It means: there are 14 hospitals which have between 1.5 and 1.6 patients per nurse.

And what of the blob at the foot of the column to the right of 1.8? This is St Sebastian's Hospital. It shows that St Sebastian's is one of five hospitals having between 1.8 and 1.9 patients for every nurse employed; it also shows how many hospitals had a worse ratio than this: twelve, to be precise.

3 Historical profile

Figure 20 (page 96) shows the historical profile of patients per nurse at St Sebastian's since 1970. Now look back and compare it with Figure 17 (page 91). This demonstrated a marked improvement from 1970 onwards. Yet here is a diagram showing the very opposite: a relentless move from the left-hand – 'good' – side of the percentile bar into the box containing the poorest 15 per cent. Which one is correct?

They are both correct, because both are accurate: nor is this an example of statistical jiggery-pokery.

The chairman's report is accurate, because the proportion of nurses to patients really did improve as shown; and Figure 20 is accurate, because although St Sebastian's was improving their nurse:patient ratios, so too were all the other mental handicap hospitals, most of them at a better rate than St Sebastian's. So St Sebastian's relative position deteriorated.

95/Comparisons between districts

Figure 20 St Sebastian's Hospital
Patients per nurse: an historical profile of performance 1970-1982

YEAR	NO OF HOSPITALS IN SAMPLE	ST. SEBASTIAN'S PATIENTS PER NURSE
1970	69	3.35
1971	69	3.03
1972	71	2.69
1973	68	2.61
1974	69	2.60
1975	71	2.22
1976	71	2.24
1977	93	2.09
1978	93	2.01
1979	94	1.99
1980	94	1.96
1981	97	1.80
1982	100	1.81

POSITION RELATIVE TO OTHER MENTAL HANDICAP HOSPITALS*

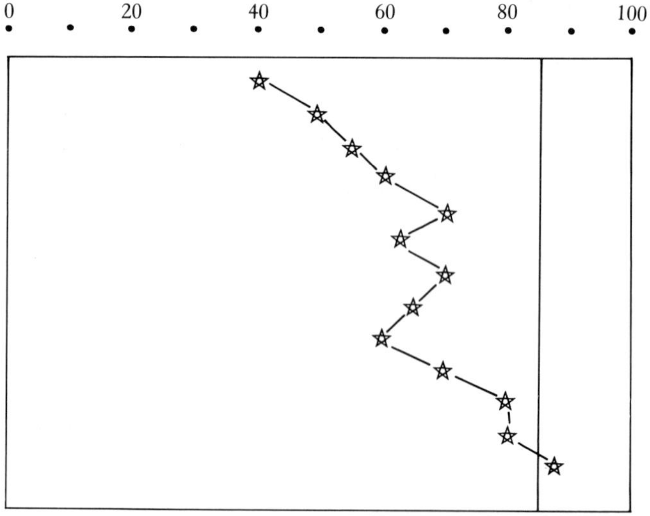

COMMENTS

This diagram displays a disturbing trend. Although the patient nurse ratio has steadily improved from 3.35 in 1970 to 1.81 in 1982, St. Sebastian's has very slowly moved from a hospital with better than average staffing levels to one which is now one of the worst staffed hospitals in England.

*The diagram shows the position of the hospital in relation to all others in the sample. The hospital with the highest number of patients per nurse would appear on the far right hand side of the diagram and the hospital with the lowest number of patients per nurse would appear on the left.
The vertical line drawn through the diagram at the 85% mark draws attention to the fact that positions to the right of that line might possibly give cause for concern.

22 NOVEMBER 1983

There is a vitally important moral in this story: never be satisfied with figures relating to your own district alone. Even though they may show a marked improvement over time, they may be nothing to write home about if every other district is improving as well.

The authority in this particular illustration found the profiles, histograms and commentaries extremely useful in dealing with their near-crisis, and once this had settled down they went on to look at the information covering their mental illness hospital and also the acute specialties so far included in the project. Indeed, they found so much of interest in what they received that they decided to invest in a small micro-computer, and to obtain the floppy disks containing all the information put together at the Health Services Management Centre; and although they themselves have decided to have information only about indicators falling in the 'worst 15 per cent' box of the profiles, their district and unit management teams receive all the information, as do the district's clinical staff.

Conclusion

Judgments about the quality of a service involve careful observation by people who know what to look for. But those who believe that statistical information has no contribution to make are depriving themselves of a valuable means of checking the evidence of their eyes and ears.

Performance indicators have repeatedly shown their effectiveness in giving advance warning of potential problems and crises. Unlike most statistical data, they are available ready processed and in a form that can be quickly understood. What is more, they are obtainable without charge!

Can you think of any reason for *not* seeing what they have to say about the services in *your* district?

Finally, notice what is special about performance indicators: not simply that they use statistical information, but that they use it in a way that illustrates clearly what is going on. If all the information you receive comes in a form that can be understood quickly and readily you will soon find that you have a deeper understanding of your district and of its challenges, its stresses and its achievements.

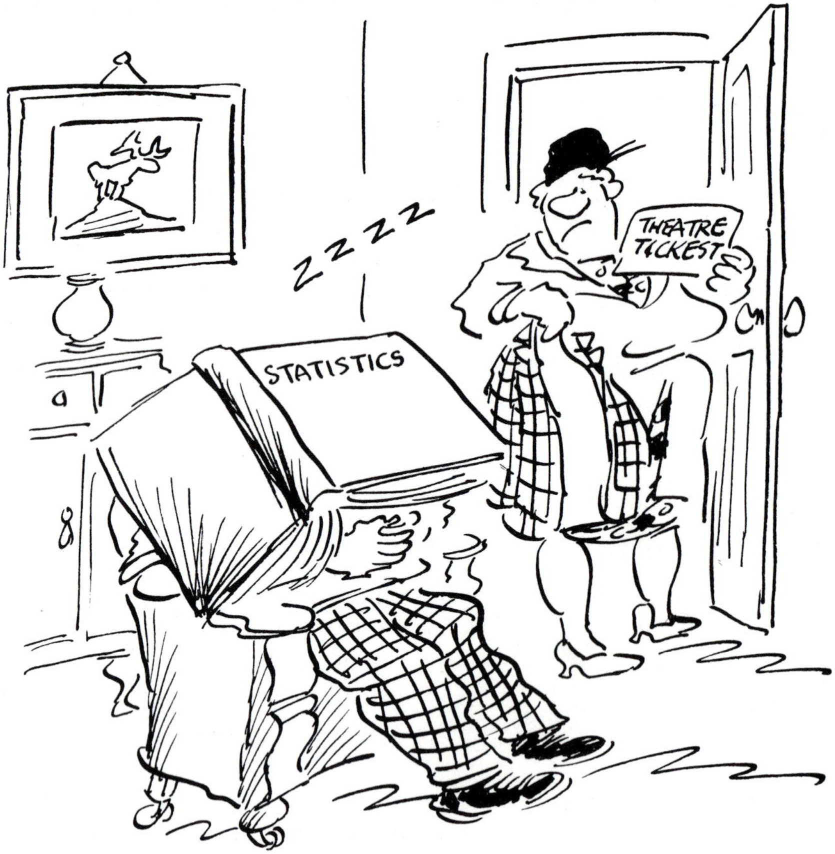
ZZZZ
STATISTICS
THEATRE TICKEST

CHAPTER SEVEN

Seduced by statistics: a cautionary tale

A recurring theme throughout this book has been the need for authorities to make intelligent and purposeful use of statistical information.

This chapter is different from the previous ones. It is about an authority which, faced with a growing problem, received a report containing – by the standards of many health authority reports – a whole galaxy of statistics. The authority accepted the report's recommendations without unfortunately noticing that the problem had not been properly understood, that certain vitally important figures had been left out and that the most important test of all had not been applied to the proposed solutions.

The problem concerned a small eye hospital which in three years had gone from coping comfortably with its annual workload to having outpatients waiting over a year to be seen by a consultant, with two or three hundred patients waiting to be admitted. The report which you will shortly be reading was written in response to the authority's concern to get the hospital back on course as quickly as possible.

But first, a word of advice. If you have found the previous chapters heavy going, they are nothing compared with what is to follow! The points are complex; there is more about figures and their analysis, and a fair amount of concentration is needed. But it is worthwhile to persevere, because you will see how very easily an authority can be swayed by the mere presence of statistics into making an inappropriate decision.

Now read the report, paying particular attention to the statistics in its appendix, and consider how you would have responded to its recommendations if it had been presented to your authority.

PILBURY HEALTH AUTHORITY
Ophthalmology Services

Patients awaiting routine outpatient appointments are currently waiting in excess of 50 weeks, a waiting time considerably longer than for any other specialty.

In addition, there are 241 patients on the waiting list for admission.

The position of waiting times for both outpatient and inpatient care has steadily deteriorated over the last 2-3 years, yet the physical resources available (theatre time, outpatient facilities and beds) are not fully utilised.

Currently there are two maximum part-time consultant ophthalmologists and one senior house officer, resulting in each consultant being first 'on call' on at least a one in three basis, allowing for cover for the SHO and each other during leave periods. Both consultants are concerned about the personal commitment necessary to maintain the service, including the casualty service at the Eye Hospital.

Encouragement is given to general practitioners to join the consultant team as clinical assistants. Previous attempts to attract general practitioners with ophthalmic training have, however, proved disappointing.

Existing consultants who are under pressure to maintain the present level of service cannot provide the necessary training time for a clinical assistant. The appointment of a further consultant would be necessary to allow a general practitioner to be employed as a clinical assistant and be adequately trained.

Proposed solution to achieve better utilisation of facilities and reduce waiting times

	£
Appoint locum consultant (short-term)	24 000
Offer 3 GP clinical assistant sessions	4 000
Appoint 2.5 WTE nurses to support above appointments	15 500
Additional cost of increased workload	5 000
	£48 500

Recommendations

1 The above appointments be made and the anticipated reduction in waiting time and increased bed occupancy stemming from them be monitored and progress reviewed in six months from implementation.

2 This retrospective appraisal should also examine the permanent staffing levels required to maintain the waiting lists at acceptably low levels.

Appendix: statistical tables

Table A Outpatients

Year	Total OPs	New OPs	Clinic sessions	New OPs per session
1980	7200	2291	292	7.8
1981	7413	2464	306	8.1
1982	7135	2466	320	7.7
1980-82 average	7269	2407	306	7.9

Outpatients waiting to be seen 550
Clinic sessions required to clear waiting list 550 divided by 7.9 per session = 70 sessions

Table B Inpatients

Year	Available	Occupied	Bed occupancy %	Discharge & deaths	Length of stay days
1980	18	7.9	43.9	502	5.8
1981	18	7.9	43.9	486	5.9
1982	18	7.0	38.9	470	5.7
1980-82 average	18	7.6	42.2	486	5.8

Table C Inpatient:outpatient ratios

Year	New OPs	Admissions	Admissions per 100 new OPs
1980	2291	502	21.9
1981	2464	486	19.7
1982	2466	470	19.1
1980-82 average	2407	486	20.2

Number of IP cases generated by 550 new OPs = $\frac{550 \times 20.2}{100} = 111$

Table D Potential average occupancy level

Average number of admissions per year		486
Backlog:		
Waiting list cases	241	
IP cases generated by 550 new OPs (from Table C, footnote)	111	
		352
Admissions required to clear backlog in one year		838

Total available bed days 18 beds × 365 days = 6570 bed days
Potential occupied bed days 838 patients × 5.8 days = 4860 bed days
Therefore potential bed occupancy 4860 divided by 6570 = 74%

The Authority's response

The members of the authority were very pleased with the report, and understandably. That alarming backlog of patients, nicely cleared in twelve months, and all for a once-only cost of under £50 000 which they just happened to have available. And how helpful to have those tables, showing that the hospital could cope so easily with it all!

They readily agreed that the recommendations should be put into effect.

Commentary

This report makes considerable use of statistical information in arriving at its proposals. Can the adequacy of those proposals be assessed? Should anything more have been done, or anything different?

Chapter One stressed the importance of structuring your approach to the things you want to know. Here are some questions that can usefully be applied to an individual problem and to the proposals put forward to solve it:

1 What is the basic problem?
2 What is its size?
3 What is its cause?
4 What is the intended outcome?
5 How can this outcome be achieved?

The next part of this chapter is in three sections:

Section 1 considers the approach of the report;

Section 2 reconsiders the basic problem;

Section 3 concludes by reflecting on the lessons to be learnt from this chapter about the place of statistics in management.

Section 1   The approach of the report

The report sees the problem as one of backlog: outpatients waiting up to 50 weeks for a first appointment; 241 patients awaiting admission. The cause is not considered. The solution is the appointment of 1.3 medical staff for a temporary period (by implication, one year). The outcome is seen as being a reduction of waiting times and an increase in bed occupancy (recommendation 1, page 100).

This section looks at the figures in terms of the report's view of the problem in three parts:

1 The outpatient figures;
2 The inpatient figures;
3 The proposal for clearing the backlog.

1 The outpatient figures
The report says two things about outpatient waiting:

1 Waiting time of routine patients for first appointment: 50 weeks (Report, para 1, page 100);
2 Number of patients awaiting a first appointment: 550 (Table A, footnote, page 101).

Now look again at Table A (page 101). Note how many new outpatients are seen in a year: around 2400, which is 200 per month. If 200 are seen every month, the 550 now waiting can surely all be seen in less than three months. Why, then, the reference to a 50-week wait?

Of course, there is no great mystery. As the report states, only routine, non-urgent, patients are waiting this long. Urgent cases are clearly lengthening the waiting time of the non-urgent cases in the way described earlier in this book (Chapter Two).

Unfortunately the report does not say anything about the waiting time for urgent cases, nor does it say how many patients are being referred as urgent. Even so, it is quite possible to make an informed guess.

Suppose that the ophthalmologists see all urgent cases within one month. In the next month 200 patients will be seen (because 200 are seen every month), including all the urgent cases. Deduct these 200 from the waiting list total of 550: this leaves 350, all non-urgent, to be seen in the following eleven months (remember: 'routine patients are waiting in excess of 50 weeks'). Eleven months, 350 patients: about 32 per month.

Conclusion: of the 200 patients seen each month, around 32 are non-urgent, leaving 168 as urgent. Put another way, out of every six outpatients, five are seen within a month and one is seen after waiting a year.

This has not altered the seriousness of the problem, but it has put a different perspective on the opening statement of the report. Had you formed the impression that patients were generally having to wait about a year to be seen in outpatients? Most people would, and the authority probably did.

2 The inpatient figures

There are 241 patients on the waiting list (Report, para 2, page 100). What does this signify in terms of waiting *time?* Since about 480 patients are admitted every year it should be possible – other things being equal – to clear a waiting list of half that number in six months.

But other things are most unlikely to be equal. It is already clear that outpatients are classified as either urgent or routine, and it would be surprising if patients awaiting admission were not classified in the same way; in addition, there are almost sure to be patients admitted as emergency cases who by-pass the outpatient department completely.

All this is guesswork, but it is sound enough to indicate that the waiting list figure is quite useless as a means of telling how long patients are having to wait to be admitted. It is no more than a figure standing in splendid isolation, and all that can be inferred is that it was once smaller and is now larger than it ought to be.

Now put this objection – fundamental though it is – to one side and look carefully again at Table D (page 101). Here the backlog is defined:

Waiting list cases	241
IP cases generated by 550 new OPs (from Table C, footnote)	111
	352

Assuming that the calculation producing those 111 patients is correct (about which more shortly), this is indeed the outstanding workload.

But is that the same as the backlog?

Consider what would be the situation if the medical staff dealt with every one of these patients as well as all the patients currently being referred to them: there would be no one on the waiting list at all. And that situation, for the reasons described in Chapter Two, is simply not tenable.

A sensible definition of backlog is not simply the outstanding workload, but the outstanding workload, less the number of patients on waiting lists short enough to produce reasonable waiting times.

In the context of this report, for example, it might be thought reasonable for a new outpatient to wait a fortnight and for a patient referred for admission to wait a month. About 100 new outpatients are seen in a fortnight and 40 patients are admitted in a month: deduct these figures from those in the report and a different picture emerges of the backlog:

	Outstanding workload	Deduction	Backlog
New outpatients	550	100	450
Waiting list cases	241	40	201
IPs generated by 450 new OPs			91
			292

Fine: a backlog of 60 fewer patients than the report would have us believe. But what of that calculation in Table C that produces 111 inpatients from 550 outpatients?

Look again at Table C. Here it is:

Table C Inpatient:outpatient ratios

Year	New OPs	Admissions	Admissions per 100 new OPs
1980	2291	502	21.9
1981	2464	486	19.7
1982	2466	470	19.1
1980-82 average	2407	486	20.2

Number of IP cases generated by 550 new OPs = $\frac{550 \times 20.2}{100}$ = 111

Each year, it seems, fewer patients are being referred for admission for every hundred seen in outpatients. But is this really the case?

No, it is not. Fewer patients are being *admitted,* but that is not the same thing as *referrals* for admission, as it ignores the fact that the waiting list is lengthening. To calculate the rate of referral correctly the number of new outpatients should be related, not to admissions, but to the number of patients actually placed on the waiting list. So that figure of 111 is almost certainly an under-estimate: how much of one we cannot tell, because the report does not give any information either about referrals or about the growth of the waiting list.

There is a second, equally serious, potential cause of error in relating admissions to new outpatients: it assumes that every patient is admitted after being seen in an outpatient clinic, when it is very likely that some are admitted direct.

So the report has – unintentionally, to be sure – misled the authority in four ways:

by presenting the waiting list as a gross total, without explanation;

by confusing outstanding workload with backlog;

by using the wrong figures to calculate the proportion of outpatients put on the waiting list for admission;

by implying that this proportion is declining.

3   The proposal for clearing the backlog
Table D (page 101) shows that the backlog can be cleared without undue pressure on the hospital's beds: an occupancy of 74 per cent for one year.

This is fine, but is it the whole story?

According to the report, the hospital's *physical* resources are not the problem (para 3, page 100): the need is for increased *staffing* resources, specifically medical staff. There are now three ophthalmologists (Report, para 4, page 100); the recommendation: increase this to 4.3 for one year (recommendation 1, page 100).

Now reconsider Table D, but in terms of medical staff instead of beds. In one year the three existing staff treat 486 inpatients: average, 162 patients per clinician. The backlog is at least 300, with 1.3 temporary clinicians to clear it: average, about 230 patients per temporary clinician. Just how realistic is it to expect these temporary additional staff to treat some 70 patients per clinician more than the permanent staff are able to treat?

It is only too clear that the proposals will not go far towards clearing the backlog, especially as the temporary staff are unlikely to be as productive as the permanent staff, whose own productivity will be cut by the need for them to train the part-time clinical assistant (Report, para 6, page 100).

But do we even now have the full picture? What are the chances that during the year when this backlog is being tackled a new backlog is building up? Could it not be that the report has become so concerned about the backlog that it has pushed to one side the crucial question: what is causing the basic problem?

Section 2   The basic problem reconsidered

The problem was seen in the report as one of backlog. The cause of the backlog was not considered, though the report mentions a deterioration in waiting times over the previous two to three years (Report, para 3, page 100).

Waiting times increase when a discrepancy occurs between demand for a service and the resources available to meet that demand, as Chapter Two explained.

Consider the report. How has this discrepancy occurred? Has demand increased? Have the resources diminished? Or have both these things happened?

The statistics say a fair amount about *activity* in the hospital during the last three years. What do they say of *demand?* How should demand on hospital facilities be measured?

The best available measure of demand is referrals, whether from general practitioners to hospital or from outpatients to the admission list, whether as emergencies, urgent cases or routine referrals. And in this particular case it is crucially important for the authority to know how many patients are being referred to the hospital. They are not told.

What can be gathered about *resources* from the report? It seems that the resources of theatre time, outpatient facilities and beds are more than enough (Report, para 3, page 100); and Table B (page 101) confirms just how under-used the beds are: you can calculate from it that the beds are empty for almost eight days on average between patients.

What of staff and finance? Is it safe to assume that the report would have mentioned any reductions in these resources if they had occurred?

Perhaps, perhaps not. All that can be said with certainty is that in its preoccupation with tackling the backlog, the report has lost sight of the need to establish its cause, simply confining itself to proposing that 'a retrospective appraisal should examine the permanent staffing levels required to maintain the waiting lists at acceptably low levels' (Report, recommendation 2, page 100). How much more satisfactory it would have been to appraise *before* plunging in with £50 000-worth of expenditure!

And why not? A few easily available statistics are all the authority needed, going back to

108/*From figures to facts* the last year or two when output kept pace with demand. They might have looked like Figure 21.

Notice how such a diagram immediately pinpoints the cause of the backlog: demand has increased while the resources of medical staff have stood still. It is also clear that unless a sudden reversal of the trend occurs, the temporary solution proposed in the report will be even more inadequate than it appeared to be in the previous section of this chapter.

What must now be found, and found quickly, are the reasons for this dramatic increase in order that future demand may be forecast and a long-term solution agreed.

While this search goes on, the authority can examine how the output of the hospital compares with that of the specialty in general. It is a sensitive issue because it can be taken as questioning whether the medical staff are pulling their weight. There could be several quite legitimate reasons for low output, however (such as poor working conditions, or obsolete equipment), some of which could be remedied without very much difficulty.

Figure 21 Eye Hospital
Referrals and medical staff, 1978-1982

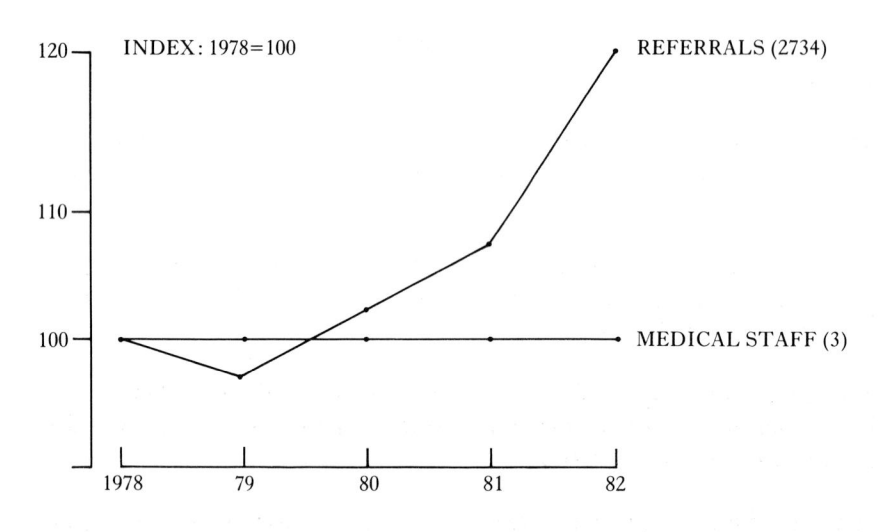

[Line graph: INDEX: 1978=100, y-axis from 100 to 120, x-axis years 1978-82. REFERRALS (2734) rises to ~120 by 1982; MEDICAL STAFF (3) remains flat at 100.]

(1982 FIGURES GIVEN IN BRACKETS)

In fact, a DHSS publication, *Health and Personal Social Statistics for England*, sent every year to all authorities in England, shows that medical staff were treating more patients than average in 1980, the most recent year for which figures are available (see Table 12).

Table 12 Ophthalmology inpatients treated per wte medical staff, 1980

	Patients treated	wte medical staff	Patients treated per wte medical staff
England	132,700*	877.9**	151
Pilbury District	502	3.0	167

* Health and Personal Social Statistics for England, 1981, Table 4.5
** Health and Personal Social Statistics for England, 1981, Table 3.7

The authority could also have seen in greater detail how their hospital compared with other ophthalmic units in England by obtaining the performance indicators described in Chapter Six.

Section 3 Conclusions

What can be learnt from this chapter?

There is no reason to doubt that the report was a conscientious attempt to come to terms with a problem. How did it so manifestly fail to do so?

1 The problem was seen in terms of its presenting symptom, a backlog, rather than its underlying cause, an increasing demand unmatched by appropriate resources to meet it.

2 The focus of concern was that patients were having to wait longer and longer to be seen and treated; but the report contained only a few scattered statistics about *current* waiting times and lists and no analysis of causes or trends.

3 The excessive waiting was correctly attributed to an insufficiency of medical staff, but the proposed solution was analysed in terms of available bed capacity, not the capacity of the medical staff to cope with the demand.

4 Having overlooked that the basic problem was a discrepancy between resources and demand, the report included no statistical information about either of these factors.

5 The report made no attempt to compare the hospital's workload with workload in the specialty in other districts.

Relevant statistical information was thus vital to all aspects of this problem and the search for its solution. The report contained more statistics than do many such reports, sufficient indeed to beguile the authority into accepting its recommendations; but the crucial ones were missing.

The moral is a simple one: statistical information is an aid to intelligent and purposeful managerial analysis, not a substitute for it.

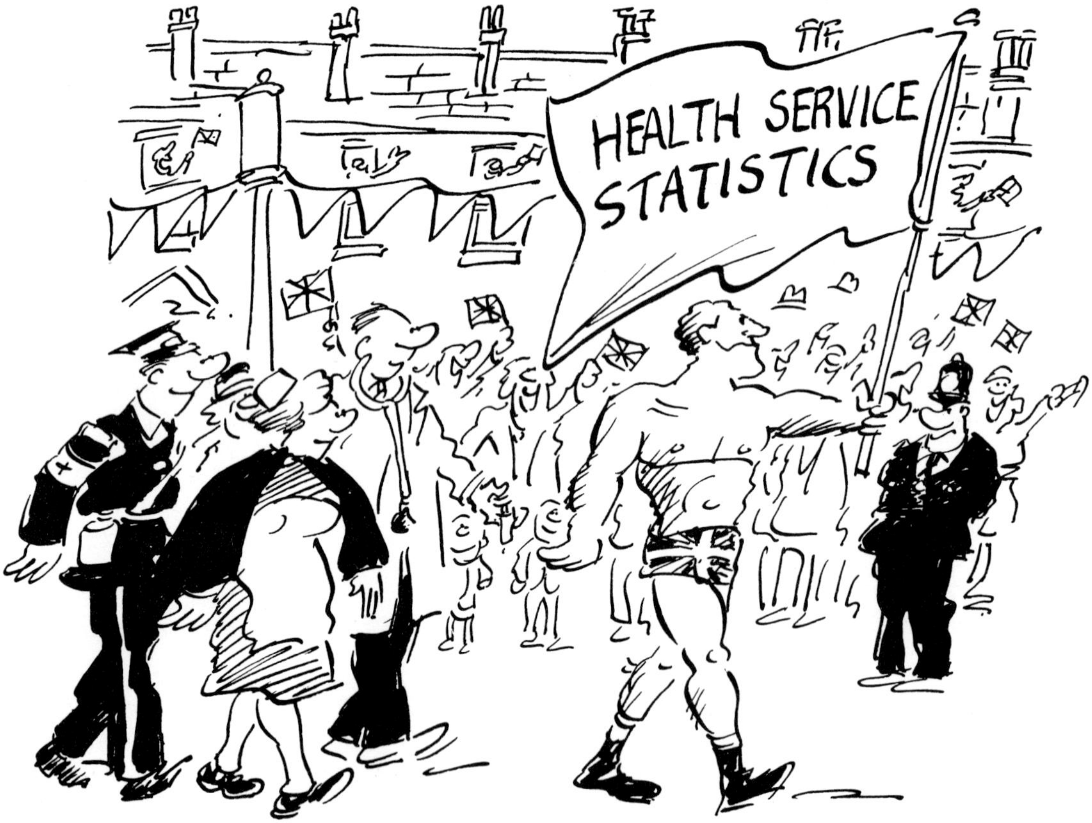
HEALTH SERVICE STATISTICS

CHAPTER EIGHT

Words into actions

Congratulations on staying the course to this last chapter, especially if you have absorbed all the complexities, homilies, injunctions and awful warnings so far. Even though some of the more obscure points of Chapter Seven may have defeated you, do not despair: they entailed a far more intense degree of analysis than you are ever likely to need – or have the time – to apply.

This chapter is in two sections, each of which looks to the future, though in different ways.

Section 1 tells you briefly about the Information Steering Group and the work they are doing to bring about vital improvements in the quality of statistical information in the health service.

Section 2 describes how you can go about making use of the information that already exists.

Section 1   The Information Steering Group

There have been many references in this booklet to the Körner Group, and you are almost sure to have heard your officers referring to it.

Its full title is the NHS/DHSS Steering Group on Health Services Information (often abbreviated to 'Information Steering Group'). Set up in 1980, it consists of about 16 senior NHS and DHSS staff initially under the chairmanship of Mrs Edith Körner, a former RHA vice-chairman. It has the huge task of reviewing all the information systems in the health service and recommending changes. It has published six reports covering the information a district requires about clinical activity in hospitals and in the community, health services manpower, patient transport services and finance. Its proposals are likely to have a radical effect on the use of statistical information in the health service.

What the Steering Group found
The Steering Group found a great deal of confusion.

Much of the statistical information was being collected and analysed as it had been in the earliest days of the NHS. True, minor alterations had been made over the years, but they had failed to take proper account of the really fundamental change that had occurred in the service: the method of delivery of health care. To take acute hospitals in particular, the statistics still assumed that a patient was admitted to one of a fixed number of specialist beds, received treatment there for some days or weeks and then went home. Flexibility in the number and location of the beds in a specialty, day cases, transfers between specialties, five-day wards, repeated admissions and so on could not be properly acknowledged, and this produced the sort of inaccuracies and distortions noted particularly in Chapter Three.

Added to this, various new statistical returns had been introduced over the years which overlapped and duplicated the information already being collected.

The Steering Group also found that people were very hazy about the purpose of collecting the statistics. Was it to help clinicians with the management of their patients? Or to help with the general management of the various services? Or to feed figures to some obscure outside body? Most staff seemed to believe that although statistical information was probably of value to others, it was not relevant to their own particular needs.

Misunderstandings about the way to record the data produced yet another problem. Most of the forms came with copious notes about how to complete them, but they were not always easy to follow, and the people who had the job of filling in the forms were often junior clerks with only a limited understanding of the intricacies of the health service. This meant that nobody could be at all sure that like was being compared with like.

Finally, because statistical information was generally viewed as being relatively unimportant, it was often inaccurate and available too late to be of any practical use.

Underlying all the Steering Group's work is their determination to overcome these problems and deficiencies.

Purpose
The Steering Group states squarely that it is concerned with the information needed by a district health authority and its managers to manage the health services.

This does not exclude its use for other purposes: far from it. It can be used as the basis for any other information systems which a district health authority or its staff may wish to develop, including clinical and epidemiological systems, and the Steering Group hopes and expects that there will be many such developments.

The Group stresses one point in particular: that health authorities and their officers who do not use the information it recommends will be 'handicapped by being inadequately informed when fulfilling their responsibilities'. Information is not an optional extra to be used or not used as you choose. You ignore it at your peril!

Content
The Group could have approached their work by analysing the philosophies, ideals and aspirations inherent in the provision of health care and developed an information system from there.

Instead they have adopted a more practical approach. Every district, they say, should collect the data which, on the basis of our knowledge and experience, we believe is necessary for the purpose of management: we will call that the minimium data set; and districts that wish to collect more than this minimum should be free to do so.

Do not be deceived by the word 'minimum' into thinking that only a modest amount of information will be involved. It will be considerable.

Naturally, you will have to be selective about what you see if you are not to be suffocated under it all, and you are likely to use exception reporting techniques to ensure that you receive early warning of potentially worrying developments.

Accuracy and timeliness
The Group has particularly stressed that figures should be accurate and also timely, by which they mean, available to the authority within six weeks of the period they relate to.

One of the best ways of ensuring accuracy is simply by making use of the figures: there is precious little incentive to bother about them if they disappear for ever into the wide blue yonder; but it is quite another matter if they rapidly surface again.

The Steering Group has adopted another principle which has the effect of improving the accuracy and timeliness of the figures: that as far as possible data needed for statistical

116/*From figures to facts*

purposes should be gathered as a by-product of the system for collecting the information for operational purposes.

A computer makes this a very straightforward process: it can be programmed to collect millions of different items of basic information, sort through them, select what is needed and analyse and present it infinitely more quickly and accurately than any human. Indeed, it is a happy coincidence that the Steering Group is working at a time when information technology is advancing so rapidly, as this is allowing it to be far more ambitious than it might otherwise have been.

Longer term aims
The Steering Group has its eyes set firmly on one particular goal: relating the activities occurring within a district to the resources of staff, money, buildings and equipment used to support those activities, the idea embodied in the phrase 'value for money'. This will happen as the Group's reports on its separate areas of activity start being brought together 'like a well made jigsaw', to quote from their report.

Awareness
The Steering Group points out the need to create an atmosphere which will encourage the staff who collect information to do so efficiently and the managers (authority members included) to use it intelligently and purposefully. It recommends that training and education should be given, and as a first stage in the process it has prepared a video film about using information in the health service.

The long history of under-use of statistics in the service means that there is a great deal of leeway to make up. Few managers these days are in the habit of using statistical information as an aid to decision making, and that habit has to be learnt again if proper use is to be made of the very extensive information advocated by the Steering Group.

But it is not really a problem. Most managers are only too well aware of the need to make better use of information and are frustrated by the limitations imposed on them by the existing systems.

Health service management has the key to vastly improved decision making within its grasp. It is vitally important that members of health authorities take the lead by understanding for themselves the essential place of sound, relevant information in the management process and insisting that intelligent use be made of it whenever decisions have to be made.

Section 2 What you can do

You may feel tempted to sit tight and do nothing until the new systems come in, especially after reading the previous few pages.

That would be a great mistake. The present systems undeniably have their faults, but these are well understood, and it is quite possible to take account of them when you study the information they produce. So do not succumb to the mañana syndrome, but make up your mind to make good use of what exists.

Reflect on two particular points which you may have noticed as you have read this book.

The first is that all the statistical information described in the book is virtually certain to be collected and available within your district, along with a great deal more besides.

The second is that there is really nothing in the least obscure or complicated about what has been described. You have only to invest your natural common sense and clear thinking in the various ideas contained here, and the return on your investment will be a far clearer understanding of what is going on.

So where do you begin? Ideally, by going through that exercise described in Chapter One with your fellow members and chief officers: thinking in an orderly fashion about what it is you want to know.

Some authorities have done this, and they have been amazed and delighted with the results: unconstrained by a formal agenda they have found themselves considering, as never before, what the issues are that really matter and just how to become better informed about them. Not that it has all been plain sailing: they have had setbacks and frustrations as they have found that the information they want is not available, or is too extensive for them to absorb, or is beyond the capacity of their staff to produce, or has proved not to give them the expected insight into a problem. But they have persevered, and they have found their efforts well worthwhile.

If you cannot persuade your authority as a whole of the advantages of making more use of statistical information, you may still find that there is enough interest among some members for you to form a small group with a special responsibility for looking at 'the figures'. Some authorities have appointed working groups or sub-committees for this purpose, and these perform a valuable role in keeping an eye on what is going on and alerting their authorities to potential problems.

If no fellow member shares your interest, on no account give up. Tell your chief officers of your interest. It will be surprising if they are not just as interested as you are, and they will probably be keen for you to talk to the staff responsible for assembling and analysing the information collected in the district. You will probably be shown computers and the very clever things they can do to display information, analyse trends, make comparisons and so on.

Enquire about performance indicators, and you may well find the staff familiar with the work of John Yates described in Chapter Six. Ask to see the figures for your district and also the performance indicators produced by the DHSS, and have their strengths and weaknesses explained to you. Discuss alternative ways of presenting whatever statistics your authority may be receiving: unless you are very unlucky, you will find the staff enthusiastic about their work and receptive to new ideas. It will not be long before you find that you have a sharper picture of your district's problems and that you can make a distinctive contribution to your authority's discussions.

Deepening your knowledge

If this book has left you keen for more, there are two things you can do.

Firstly, you can read more books. Two have been mentioned earlier (pages 23 and 55); another highly relevant and interesting one is *Using Numbers for Effective Health Service Management,* by Mike Tyrrell (Heinemann 1975). Your officers may well suggest others to you: there is certainly no shortage of them.

Secondly, you can take part in the seminars for members put on by regional health authorities and by the university departments, colleges, polytechnics and other seats of learning with health service connections. In some cases the lecturers concerned will lay something on locally for a specific authority, council or voluntary body, with their information needs particularly in mind, and will follow this up with an advisory service, if required.

A last Reminder

This book has aimed to give you some ideas about how to use information constructively in the health service. The more you use those ideas, the more they will come as second nature to you.

Some basic principles have cropped up many times. Always have them in mind when you are choosing and using information. Some people find it helpful to work systematically through a set of questions such as these:

When choosing statistics	*When using statistics*
What do I want to know?	Is this what I want to know?
Why?	Why?
What can give me this knowledge?	Does it tell me what I need to know?
What use do I intend to make of it?	What action should I take on it?
How do I want it presented to me?	Is it being presented clearly to me?
How can I compare it?	How does it compare?
How often do I want to see it?	Should I be seeing it more often, or less?
When should I review what I see?	Do I still want to see it?

This book can take you only so far. It is up to you now to make full use of information and thereby enhance your knowledge of what is going on and improve the quality of the decisions you make. And may all your endeavours meet with unqualified success!

POSTSCRIPT

Figures, facts and general management

During the preparation of this book the NHS Management Inquiry Report – 'Griffiths' – was published and the Government decided to put its recommendations into effect.

How do those recommendations relate to the themes of the book?

The Griffiths report stresses the need for the centre to show that it is 'passionately concerned about the quality of care and the delivery of services.'

As a member you are concerned above all that the services provided in your authority's name should be of a high quality. Such a phrase is meaningless on its own: it needs expanding, refining, qualifying. How *effective*, for example, is each of your services in meeting the purpose for which it exists? How *comprehensive* are the services, and how acceptable are those provided for you by other districts and other agencies? How *accessible* are your services, especially to those restricted by infirmity, poverty or old age? How *responsive* are they? How *compassionate* are the staff who provide them? How *efficiently* are they provided? And what exactly do you mean by quality that is *high*?

You will know from your study of this book that the answers to such questions can be expressed in specific and precise terms. You will also know that in applying itself to those answers an authority begins to develop its values, set its standards and define its objectives.

So far so good. But what purpose is served if, the authority having done those things, nothing happens? Over the years prior to 1985 many authorities had such experiences, so much so that issues of quality all but disappeared from their discussions, and such objectives as they had were vague and imprecise.

In essence, general management – the central theme of Griffiths – is all about converting what the authority *wants* to happen into what *does* happen: about putting the authority's decisions into effect and achieving its objectives.

It will take some time for the general management function to be brought into operation. Members who use that time to get to grips with what is going on in their districts and

122/From figures to facts shape up their ideas about the quality of their services will be giving the sense of direction to their district that is so vital to its progress; and the general managers who start out with a clear picture of their authorities' ideals and aspirations are those that will be most successful in making them a reality.

It may perhaps be that the years have passed and your general managers are now well established. Then consider: do you regularly receive information which allows you to assess the quality of each of your district's services? Do you carry out that assessment and, where you establish the need for improvements, do you ensure that they are achieved? Are you constantly looking ahead to ensure that the services are geared up to cope with expected changes? And when unexpected crises occur are you provided with the information you need to decide how best to tackle them?

If you can say 'yes' to all these questions, and your annual performance reviews are occasions for modest pride as the congratulations pour in, you have done well indeed. If, on the other hand, you still have some way to go, the ideas in this book should be of use to you. They are based on this very simple – and timeless – principle: the better your understanding, the higher the quality of the decisions you take.

APPENDIX A

How to calculate the four common measures of bed use

$$\text{Percentage bed occupancy} = \frac{\text{occupied beds} \times 100}{\text{available beds}}$$

$$\text{Length of stay} = \frac{\text{occupied beds} \times \text{days in period}}{\text{discharges and deaths}}$$

$$\text{Turnover interval} = \frac{(\text{available beds} - \text{occupied beds}) \times \text{days in period}}{\text{discharges and deaths}}$$

$$\text{Throughput per bed} = \frac{\text{discharges and deaths}}{\text{available beds}}$$

Example

In the period April – June (91 days) a 30-bedded ward discharged 285 patients. Each night the ward was occupied on average by 26 patients.

$$\text{Percentage bed occupancy} = \frac{26 \times 100}{30} = 86.5\%$$

$$\text{Length of stay} = \frac{26 \times 91}{285} = 8.3 \text{ days}$$

$$\text{Turnover interval} = \frac{(30-26) \times 91}{285} = 1.3 \text{ days}$$

$$\text{Throughput per bed} = \frac{285}{30} = 9.5 \text{ patients}$$

124/From figures to facts *Warning* Occasionally these figures go wrong.

Suppose that 30 of those 285 patients had been transferred to another ward and then sent home. They would then have been counted as discharges from the second ward, but not from this one.

All the calculations would then have been based on 255 discharges, not 285, and every figure except percentage bed occupancy would have been different: a longer length of stay and turnover interval, a lower throughput per bed.

It is because this sort of nonsense can happen that the Körner review of information is so urgently needed.

APPENDIX B

Calculating a measure of bed use from two known measures and depicting all four measures on a single diagram

1 The calculations

The left hand column below gives the formula for calculating the wanted measure.

To the right of the formula an example is given to show how the formula works.

The *example* is of a ward in which the length of stay is 3 days and the turnover interval is 2 days. The bed occupancy is 60% and the ward has a throughput of 73 patients per annum (365 days).

A Occupancy

$$\frac{100 \times \text{length of stay}}{\text{length of stay} + \text{turnover interval}} \qquad \frac{100 \times 3}{3 + 2} = 60\%$$

$$\frac{100 \times \text{length of stay} \times \text{throughput}}{\text{days in period}} \qquad \frac{100 \times 3 \times 73}{365} = 60\%$$

$$100\left(1 - \frac{\text{turnover interval} \times \text{throughput}}{\text{days in period}}\right) \qquad 100\left(1 - \frac{2 \times 73}{365}\right) = 60\%$$

B Throughput

$$\frac{\text{days in period}}{\text{length of stay} + \text{turnover interval}} \qquad \frac{365}{3 + 2} = 73 \text{ patients}$$

$$\frac{\text{days in period} \times \text{occupancy}}{100 \times \text{length of stay}} \qquad \frac{365 \times 60}{100 \times 3} = 73 \text{ patients}$$

$$\frac{\text{days in period} \times (100 - \text{occupancy})}{100 \times \text{turnover interval}} \qquad \frac{365 \times (100-60)}{100 \times 2} = 73 \text{ patients}$$

126/From figures to facts   C   Length of stay

$$\frac{\text{days in period}}{\text{throughput}} - \text{turnover interval} \qquad \frac{365}{73} - 2 \qquad = 3 \text{ days}$$

$$\frac{\text{turnover interval} \times \text{occupancy}}{100 - \text{occupancy}} \qquad \frac{2 \times 60}{100 - 60} \qquad = 3 \text{ days}$$

$$\frac{\text{days in period} \times \text{occupancy}}{100 \times \text{throughput}} \qquad \frac{365 \times 60}{100 \times 73} \qquad = 3 \text{ days}$$

D   Turnover interval

$$\frac{\text{days in period}}{\text{throughput}} - \text{length of stay} \qquad \frac{365}{73} - 3 \qquad = 2 \text{ days}$$

$$\frac{100 \times \text{length of stay}}{\text{occupancy}} - \text{length of stay} \qquad \frac{100 \times 3}{60} - 3 \qquad = 2 \text{ days}$$

$$\frac{\text{days in period} \times (100 - \text{occupancy})}{100 \times \text{throughput}} \qquad \frac{365 \times (100 - 60)}{100 \times 73} \qquad = 2 \text{ days}$$

2   The Barber-Johnson diagram

Ten years or so ago, two enterprising health service operational research experts, Barry Barber and David Johnson, produced a diagram which can be used to show all the four measures at the same time (see Figure 22).

You will see that the measures of *time* form the two axes of the diagram and that *occupancy* measures radiate from the point where the two axes meet. The measures of *throughput* form the hypotenuse of a triangle whose right-angle is at the point where the axes meet.

A point anywhere on this diagram is all that is now required to indicate all four of the measures of bed use.

As an example, a cross appears on the diagram. It happens to be exactly where two lines

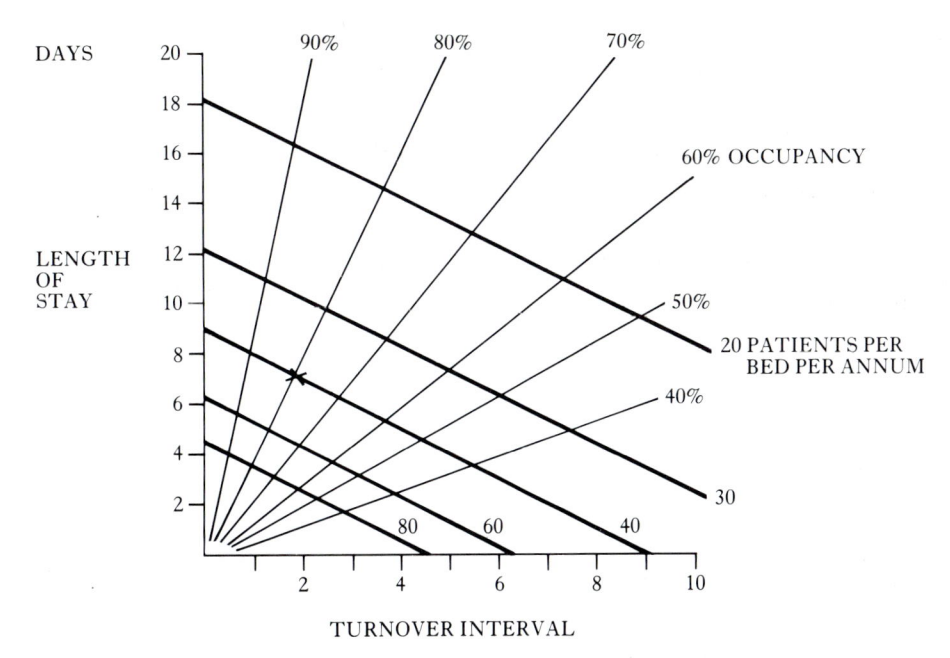

Figure 22 The Barber-Johnson diagram   *127/Appendix B*

[Barber-Johnson diagram: Length of Stay (days) on vertical axis from 2 to 20; Turnover Interval on horizontal axis from 2 to 10; occupancy lines at 90%, 80%, 70%, 60%, 50%, 40%; throughput lines at 80, 60, 40, 30, 20 patients per bed per annum]

intersect: follow one of them diagonally upwards, and you find an occupancy level of 80 per cent; follow the other diagonally to the right, and you find a throughput of 40 patients per bed per annum. Look to the left, and you find that the cross is roughly in line with a length of stay of 7¼ days; look down, and you find that the cross is directly above a turnover interval of between 1¾ and 2 days.

Notice particularly that the more intensively beds are used, the closer the cross on the diagram moves to the corner where the two axes meet (the bottom left-hand corner).

Of the many uses to which the Barber-Johnson diagram is put, perhaps one of the most interesting shows changes over time.

Figure 23 (page 128) depicts the national bed usage figures for gynaecology from 1973 to 1979.

You can see from this diagram that over the seven years there was no reduction in turnover interval, and occupancy levels deteriorated very slightly (from just over to just

128/From figures to facts   Figure 23   National bed usage figures for gynaecology, 1973-1979

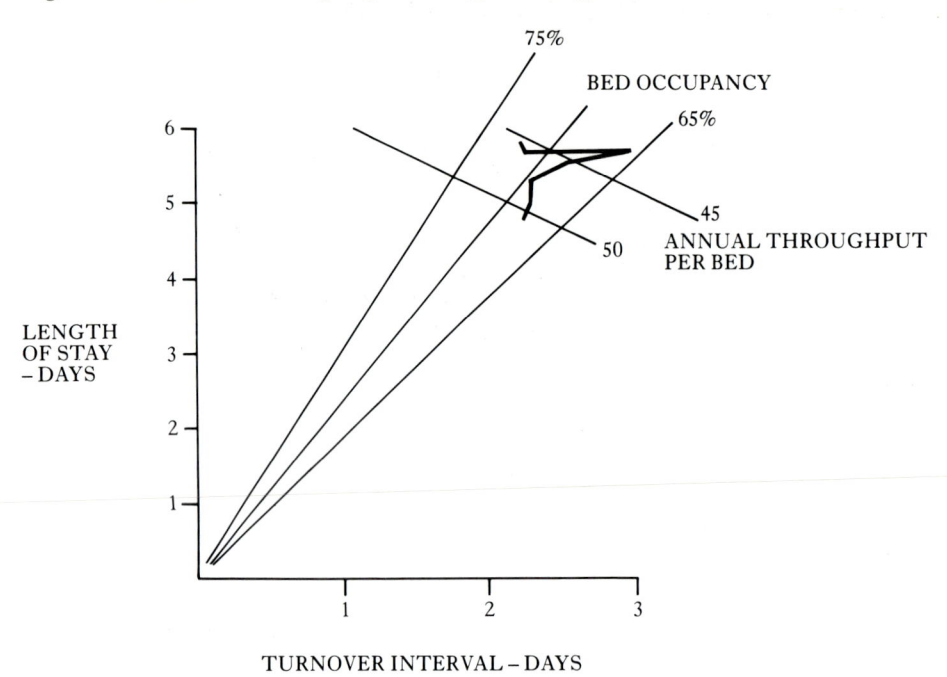

under 70 per cent); on the other hand, length of stay gradually reduced by one whole day, thereby increasing the throughput of patients to more than 50 per bed per annum.

There are two unsatisfactory features about Figure 23. First, it contains a huge amount of blank space. Second, the two axes of the graph both represent days, but the horizontal axis is twice the scale of the vertical axis. If they were both the same there would be even more blank space!

Figure 24 tackles both these objections by 'zooming in' on the important part of Figure 23 and makes the scale of the two axes the same. It also provides plenty of space to plot a district's own figures next to the national figures.

An interpretation of this diagram might read like this:

Both nationally and locally, length of stay reduced by one day, and throughput increased

Figure 24 Islan District Gynaecology
         Local and national statistics of bed utilisation, 1973-1979

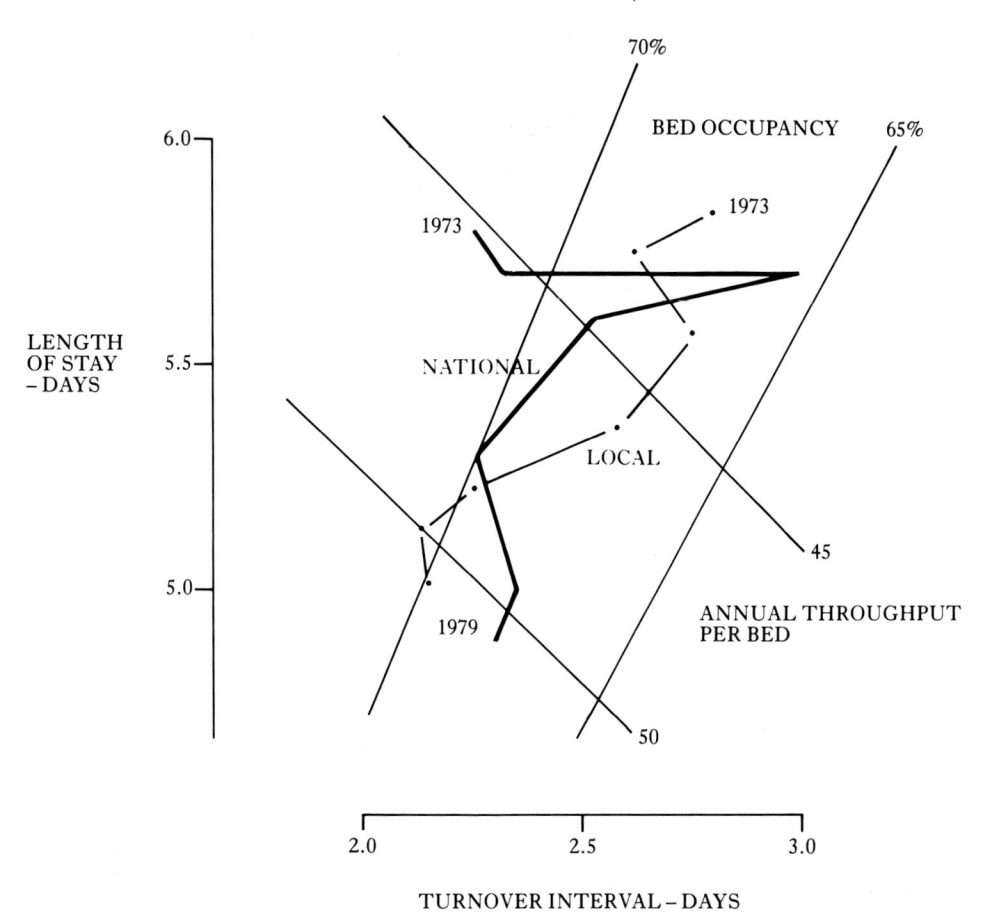

129/Appendix B

LENGTH OF STAY – DAYS

BED OCCUPANCY

ANNUAL THROUGHPUT PER BED

TURNOVER INTERVAL – DAYS

by five patients and seven patients per bed respectively, over the seven-year period.

In 1973 the local unit was using its beds far less intensively than the national average: in particular, its turnover interval was a full half-day longer. In 1974 its position improved slightly, and in 1975 the industrial action by its medical staff had a comparatively minor effect.

130/From figures to facts   By 1977 the local and national figures were very close, and in 1978 local bed use was significantly higher than nationally.

In 1979 the local unit shared with the national average a throughput of 51 patients per bed; and a slightly longer stay and shorter turnover interval meant that its occupancy level was three percentage points higher at 70 per cent.

Index

Major references in bold type

Accessibility 20
Accuracy 22, 29, 39, 115
Activity 107, 113, 116
Allocation, financial 77, 79
Analysis 12, 43, 66, 67, 86, 99, 109, 110
Annual performance reviews 122
Appraisal 100, 107
Authority, health 5, 12, 16, 17, 29, 30, 34, 115, 117, 118
Averages 23, 48, 64, 65, 93, 106
Awareness 116

Backlog 101-107, 109
Barber, D 126
Barber-Johnson diagram 44, **126-130**
Bars, percentile 92, 93, 95
Bed days 63, 101
Bed emptiness 49
Bed occupancy *see* Occupancy, bed
Bed use measures *see* Measures of bed use
Birmingham University 89, 91
British Institute of Mental Handicap 91

Calculator 10, 44, 116, 118
Capacity 11, 27, 29, 39, 40, 109
Clinical judgment 46, 48
Comparison 11, 12, 21, 24, 52, 53, 85, **89-97**, 118
Computer 9, 22, 66, 80, 116, 118
Control, manpower *see* Manpower control

Data 10, 12, 66, 74, 97
Day cases 30, 31, 32, 44, 46, 47, 54, 64, 114
Definitions 23
Demand 11, 15, 19, 27, 29, 39, 40, 46, 79, 107, 108, 109
Department of Health and Social Security 89
Development Team for Mentally Handicapped 91
Display 22
Distribution 86, 95
Drift 80

Effectiveness 77, **84-86**, 89, 97
Efficiency 71, **81-84**
Elimination 20
Emergency 19, 29, 31, 32, 39, 48, 104
Emptiness, bed 49
Establishments 77-80
Expertise 21, 46
Explanations 27, 34

Finance 113
Flexibility 44, 114
Fluctuations 52
Formulae 10
Frequency diagram 95

Griffiths Report 121

Health and Personal Social Statistics 109
Health authorities *see* Authorities, health
Health Services Management Centre 89, 91

132/From figures to facts

Histograms 92, 95, 96
Hostility 24
Huff, D 23

Indexes 12, **57-60**, 67
Indicators, performance *see* Performance indicators
Inferences 22
Information, statistical 5, 9, 10, 12, 16, 17, 64, 77, 97, 99, 102, 109, 110, 113, 114, 116, 117
Information Steering Group *see* Steering Group, Information
Inputs 21, 87

Jargon 12
Johnson, D 126
Judgments 24, 89
Jugular-funicular model, incredible 17, 18

Körner, Mrs E 5, 9, 12, 21, 33, 39, 44, 46, 80, 113, 124

Length of stay, hospital 31, 43, 44, **45-47**, 54, 63, 93, 123, 127, 128, 130
Limiting staff 77, **79-80**
Losing staff services 82

Management 5, 13, 87, 102, 114, 116, 121
Managers, general 122
Manpower control 12, 19, **77-87**
Measures of bed use 12, **43-50**, **123-130**
Members, authority 5, 9, 11, 29, 118
Micro-computer 97
Minimum data set 115

NHS/DHSS Steering Group on Health Services Information *see* Steering Group, Information
NHS Management Inquiry 121
Norms 12, 57, **64-65**, 67
Numbers, small 23

Objectives 121
Occupancy, bed 15, 23, 44, **49-50**, 51, 63, 85, 100, 101, 102, 106, 123, 126, 127, 130
Outcomes 19
Outputs 19, 21, 87, 108

Payments, unnecessary **81-82**
Percentage bed occupancy *see* Occupancy, bed
Percentile bars 92, 93, 95
Performance indicators, 9, 89, **90-97**, 109, 118
Performance reviews, annual 122
Plans 57-74
Population 17, 18, 59, 62
Projects 57-74
Presentation 11, **21**, 27, 33, 43, **50**
Profiles 92, 93, 95, 96

Quality 119, 121, 122

Rates 12, 17, 57, **60-64**, 66, 82, 83, 84, 105
Ratios 90, 91, 93, 95, 101, 105
Referrals 35, 39, 40, 66, 73, 105, 106, 107
Reporting, exception *see* Exception reporting
Resignations 82, 83
Resources 40, 107, 108, 109
Retail price index 57

Selection 11, **17**
Seminars 118
Sickness, staff 82-83, 84
Standards, setting 11, 12, 30, 41, 47, 54, 55
Statistics *see* Data; Information, statistical; Techniques
Steering Group, Information 113-116 *see also* Körner, Mrs E

Targets 64, 65
Techniques 57-74, 87
Throughput, bed 44, **50**, 123, 126, 127, 128, 130
Timeliness 22, 115
Transfers, patient 45, 114, 124
Trends 34, 52, 59, 82, 96, 109, 118
Turnover interval 23, 44, **47-48**, 54, 123, 127, 128, 130
Turnover, staff 83, 84
Tyrrell, Mike 118

Value for money 116
Variables 84

Waiting lists and times 11, 15, 19, **27-37**, 39, 54, 70, 71, 78, 99, 100, 101, 102, 103, 104, 105, 106, 107, 109

Yardsticks 65, 84, 86
Yates, John G 55, 89, 118